WOODWORKING

The Ultimate Guide to Building Creative Projects

(A Step-by-step Beginner's Guide to Woodworking and Its Techniques)

Kristi Olivarria

Published By Jackson Denver

Kristi Olivarria

All Rights Reserved

Woodworking: The Ultimate Guide to Building Creative Projects (A Step-by-step Beginner's Guide to Woodworking and Its Techniques)

ISBN 978-1-77485-345-0

All rights reserved. No part of this guide may be reproduced in any form without permission in writing from the publisher except in the case of brief quotations embodied in critical articles or reviews.

Legal & Disclaimer

The information contained in this book is not designed to replace or take the place of any form of medicine or professional medical advice. The information in this book has been provided for educational and entertainment purposes only.

The information contained in this book has been compiled from sources deemed reliable, and it is accurate to the best of the Author's knowledge; however, the Author cannot guarantee its accuracy and validity and cannot be held liable for any errors or omissions. Changes are periodically made to this book. You must consult your doctor or get professional medical advice before using any of the suggested remedies, techniques, or information in this book.

Upon using the information contained in this book, you agree to hold harmless the Author from and against any damages, costs, and expenses, including any legal fees potentially resulting from the application of any of the information provided by this guide. This disclaimer applies to any damages or injury caused by the use and application, whether directly or indirectly, of any advice or information presented, whether for breach of contract, tort, negligence, personal injury, criminal intent, or under any other cause of action.

You agree to accept all risks of using the information presented inside this book. You need to consult a professional medical practitioner in order to ensure you are both able and healthy enough to participate in this program.

TABLE OF CONTENTS

INTRODUCTION 1

CHAPTER 1: WHERE TO BEGIN WITH WOODWORKING IF YOU DON'T KNOW ANYTHING AT ALL 2

CHAPTER 2: MANUAL FOR IDENTIFYING WOOD 17

CHAPTER 3: WOODWORKING BASICS 29

CHAPTER 4: WOODWORKING STRATEGIES 39

CHAPTER 5: WOODWORKING FAIL-FREE SKILLS, TIPS AND TECHNIQUES 51

CHAPTER 6: WOODWORKING TOOLS 56

CHAPTER 7: SIMPLE DIY WOODWORKING PROJECTS 79

CHAPTER 8: SECURITY GUIDELINES WHEN UTILIZING TOOLS 105

CHAPTER 9: THE REASONS TO SHOULD YOU LEARN WOODWORKING? 113

CHAPTER 10: WOODWORKING PROJECTS YOU CAN MASTER AT HOME 118

CHAPTER 11: WHAT TO BEWARE OF/ DO'S AND DON'TS TO AVOID WHEN CHOOSING WOOD 125

CHAPTER 12: THE SMALL FURNITURE (BEGINNERS PLAN) 134

CHAPTER 13: YOU MUST HAVE PERSONAL SAFETY GEAR 149

CHAPTER 14: SIMPLE WOODWORKING PROJECTS TO START WITH 155

CHAPTER 15: ENGRAVING 159

CHAPTER 16: WOODWORKING WITH PALLETS 164

CHAPTER 17: TOOLS SHOP.. 169

CHAPTER 18: EASY WOODWORKS................................. 182

CONCLUSION... 185

Introduction

In this book, you'll discover the tried and true methods and techniques for understanding the fundamentals for woodworking i.e. to recognize the tools needed and wood to be used, develop plans for any woodwork project and perform simple woodwork tasks.

If you are able to fully read the book and implement the knowledge in this book this book will allow you gain knowledge and applications important to the field of woodworking , as described.

Chapter 1: Where to Begin With Woodworking If You Don't Know Anything at All

If you are a novice about woodworking Don't panic.This book will begin at the beginning and assume that you've got little understanding of how you can begin your journey with woodworking.This chapter will cover the basic things you'll need to start, such as the tools you must be acquiring immediately as well as the space you'll require, and the methods you'll need to learn if you think of becoming a respected woodworker.After having read this chapter, you'll know what you'll need to ensure your success.This is a good beginning point for those who are new.

Step 1 for Beginning Woodworking Success: Be aware of where you Stand

Before we look at the tools you'll need to begin woodworking, you must recognize that you shouldn't have the temptation to go out and buy a plethora of expensive tools for woodworking before you begin and finish that first project.As you'll find that you can master the fundamentals of woodworking without having to invest lots of money.If you're tempted to buy expensive equipment consider taking the time to think whether woodworking might be the right hobby for you.Without practicing and discipline, you're likely that you'll end up packing your tools and finding a place to put them into your closet to become dustier than you think.

Step 2 to a successful beginning woodworking experience Start by acquiring the basic tools you'll need

While we'll cover hand tools as well as power tools in the next article, here are some essential tools you'll require in order to start started.Let's examine these today.

Essential Tools 1:

Hammers are hammers.

-Nails

-Screws

A Screwdriver

A drill of a certain kind

The tools mentioned above may seem like common sense however the reality is that they're the only tools are required (in together using wood) to learn the fundamentals that are required in the process.If are someone that seldom picks up an hammer to attach it in a nail you'll need to get familiar with this method so that you don't risk damaging the fingers of your hands.If you're used to using the tools mentioned above, then you're welcome to purchase the next set of indispensable tools.Either you choose, it's possible that you have this type of equipment within your house.

Essential Tool 2: A Speed Square

Contrary to the tools were talked about in the last section, a speed-square might be something that you are not aware about.

As you can see from the photo above, a speed square is a small and triangularly-shaped tool.In fact, there's a chance that you may also come to know the speed square as a triangle square or a rafter square, since all three of these names are used interchangeably.Essentially, the speed square can be used as all of the following:

A method for making precise 90 and 45-degree angle cuts using hand or circular saws

A protractor is a tool to create angles quickly and with accuracy

Measurement lines need to be precisely perpendicular with the edge the wood board

For precise marking and measuring angles of 45 degrees.

In order to determine the length of the board with respect to the cut you're planning to make

As you can see from the array of functions offered by the speed-square, its principal goal is to measure lines swiftly and easy, in hopes of saving time and your self the frustration.Most speed squares are sold on the market can be found in aluminum, plastic or steel.The price of a speed-square can be anywhere from fifteen to thirty dollars. It's crucial to choose one that is of high-quality to ensure your measurements are as exact as is possible.

Essential Tools 3: Saws

There are numerous saws are available to you when you're a woodworker in the making and it's safe claim that the remainder of this guide could cover just the different kinds of saws readily available to you when you begin your craft.While we'll dive deeper in-depth about the kinds of hand saws and power saws are available for use, any saw is vital to an aspiring woodworker, especially when getting started out.Without the aid of a saw it's impossible you cut wood.How will you be able to make furniture or various other designs without cutting the wood in the future? The most popular saws used by woodworkers, which we'll go over in detail later are:

A circular saw

-A jig saw

A saw that is reciprocating

A table saw

-A miter saw

Essential Tool 4: A Clamp

A clamp is made to secure the wood when you cut it, therefore it's obvious why clamps are an essential tool for your woodworking equipment arsenal.The most simple clamp available to purchase is the C-clamp.The C-clamp can be seen below.

No matter if you have an existing woodworking table available The C-clamp can be used to attach itself to any table you're working to cut wood.These clamps are available in various sizes, with a range of four and eight inches.These clamps are priced around 15 dollars per piece, with clamps with the highest price being those that are able to accommodate larger chunks of lumber.Basically the greater the weight a C-clamp is able to be able to support the greater it's likely cost you in terms of cost.

Essential Tool 5: A Sander

If you don't want the final product to be rough with the risk of inflicting splinters on other people and splinters, then you'll need to purchase one of the sanders which will let you smooth out your wood once you've completed designing it.Sanders are, in general, are among the most expensive investments you can invest in your woodworking hobby therefore, make sure you really enjoy woodworking prior to investing on this tool.There are a variety of sanders you can purchase, and two of the most commonly used include the belt sander as well as an orbital sander.The orbital sander is likely the best choice for the designs you're planning to create like furniture or other tiny trinkets.Lastly you should know that, in addition to buying your sander, it's required invest in sandpaper.Depending on the kind of wood you're going to use in your work, you can choose from different kinds of sandpaper that will correspond to the degree of smoothness you desire.The more refined the quality of your sander smoother the final product will to be.For instance, if you intending to buy sandpaper of 120 grade that will cause your wood to be less smooth than 220 grit paper will.

Step 3 for Beginner Woodworking Success: Be aware of the space that is required

Now that you have a basic understanding of the types of tools in which you can invest that may be beneficial to you when you're first starting out woodworking, we will now move onto understanding the space constraints that a woodworking hobby requires.Unlike other types of hobbies or sports, you're likely not going to be traveling to a stadium or to a place where you will meet with a group to discuss activity plans.From this perspective, it's obvious to see that the hobby of woodworking is largely an individual or two-person endeavor.Additionally, unless you rent out space from a local storefront or other type of space arrangement, you're likely not going to be able to pursue the hobby of woodworking unless you have a lot of space readily available in your home.In general, the size of the space that you choose for your woodworking hobby should be able to fit large pieces of wood in it where you can later cut them and store them for future use. For this reason, a lot of individuals choose to set up and develop their passion in a garage, basement or a porch, driveway, or perhaps at their home's backyard.

If you also know that you'll perform a lot of sanding work, you'll need to ensure that you select the right woodworking area that is safe for dust of sanding to accrue.It's known that dust that builds up due to sanding could be harmful for the human lungs.Without getting into the details the risks that can result from inhaling massive amounts of sanding particles can result in lung scarring over the course of time and also shorter-term irritation.If you discover that you're doing frequent sanding regularly, be sure you regularly clean up your workspace and wear a mask for sanding to ensure that you don't cause any lung damage those in your vicinity.

Finally, the lighting of the room you select must be adequate for two major reasons.The primary reason is to be capable of seeing the wood your working on.How do you think you'll be in a position to mark, cut and set up your wood pieces if you're constantly looking up to ensure that your measurements are accurate? Secondly it is essential to be able to align the saw's blades precisely to the measurements you're making. This usually requires a sharp eye.For this reason, it could be wise to consider doing yourself a favor and purchase an florescent light source to illuminate your work space.Of course, if your planning to work on projects outside in your backyard in the summer when the sun is shining and you're not worried about many concerns regarding the right lighting source.

Step 4 for Beginning Woodworking Success The key to success for beginners is practice, practice, and Practice!

The final step we'll be discussing is the concept of practicing the abilities you require to acquire to complete woodworking in the correct way.To accomplish this goal it is important to be capable of assessing your development as a woodworker with an objective view and be aware of the areas in which you could have improved your skills and craft.Practicing and enhancing your skills in these areas will be beneficial to your long-term success:

• Marking your wood If you're not able to create precise markings on the wood, chances are that your work will turn out to be ugly and lopsided when you attempt to do it and you hope to succeed.When you're trying to mark your wood, apply painter's adhesive on the wood or pencil (if you do not want to write in the board itself).This is particularly helpful if you're aware that you'll need to align it in a certain direction so that the other face is "up".It's an extremely common error for woodworkers to forget to write down the side that"up "up" in their board, only for them to discover their error after they've removed their wood.Do yourself an favor and start this habit earlier rather than later.You'll be grateful for it.

Measurement isn't simple for everyone, and for those who aren't very skilled in math, it can be an daunting notion.This is why it's crucial to get used to measuring to determine your precision and the requirements to improvement.When you're just beginning your journey you might not feel that measuring is a necessity however if you decide to develop into a better woodworker, then you'll require measuring skills to finish complicated projects.If you're interested in practicing measuring, you should measure the board and record your measurements.After you've finished take the measurements you've completed with regard to your cut onto the wood that you've cut and observe what happens when it comes out.If the cut is in line with the image you imagined in your mind, then you've achieved it down.Otherwise you can go back to your drawing board until the measurement gets better.

Templates are utilized in woodworking when trying to create the same cut more than once on the same piece wood.For instance, if you are building a table with one leg that are even a tiny small bit off, then the the table will be unstable due to the particular spot.Instead of relying on yourself to make the same cuts every time, a template can aid you in making precise cuts this without worrying about human error.As an additional note, if you are aware that you'll cut using a variety of templates, you ought to think about making templates made of plywood instead of wood ones as they tend to be the most long-lasting.

Chapter 2: Manual for Identifying Wood

Be sure to ensure it's pure solid wood

It is a crucial step as it ensures that you're using the correct materials for your projects. There are many which are man-made composite or plastics that mimic wood. For confirmation, take a look at the ends of the grain to observe growth rings that are formed by the annual expansion of trees, it is important to determine if it's veneered since veneers are made with an alternating grain pattern. the other thing to check is whether it has been printed or painted to resemble wood.

Verifying the grain color

It is important to know if the grain's color is stretched or the natural color of wood. You can determine whether the wood is patinated or has weathered. When wood is exposed to the elements outside, it is likely to fade to a boring gray. Additionally, the woods in the interior can develop patinas as they age and begin to get darker. Try to plan or sand the board so that you can check the wood's natural, raw color.

Examine the grain pattern

If you're dealing with wood that has not been finished, it is possible to check the texture of your grain. This can be done by determining if the wood is porous or has an open texture. Softwoods tend to be smooth and lack grain indentations, while some common hardwoods have structures with an porous and open. It is important to know whether the wood is plain-sawn or quarter-sawn. If you check this, you can determine the way the board was made out of the wood e.g. quarter-sawn oak surfaces have the appearance of flecks. Another thing to look for is whether the wood exhibits any unique characteristic or form like sapwood or curly, wild-grain, or knots. For instance, maple is characterized by curly curves.

Verifying the strength and the weight

It is possible to determine the wood's the weight of it by lifting it and estimating its weight and taking a look at the weights of other wood species that are commonly used. You can also slash the edge of the wood with using your fingernail to estimate the hardness. You can also estimate the density of the wood using a scale to get length, width and width measurements and then combine the measurements. Then, you can examine its density against other density measurements available on the internet database.

Find out the source

Finding out the origin of the wood is extremely beneficial even if you only learn the tiniest details about the wood. The wood's age can help determine the source of the species of wood. The wood's age can allow you to determine the extent to which patina been developed, and also help to determine what species were popular at various times in the past. Another thing you can look at is the dimensions of the wood piece, trees vary in terms of size, and some may be extremely small, while others are quite large. It is important to find out what the wood was intended to be used for, and this can provide you with a clue which will assist you in identify it.

Verify the end grain

The eng-grain test is a reliable, precise and efficient method of identifying the wood. It's a reliable method that is repeatable and reliable and it is possible to check the finish-grain using an magnifier. End-grain surfaces aren't as easy to work with or cooperative like face grain surfaces, so you need to strive to get a smooth and clean end-grain. It is possible to use a sharp knife or razor to slice a piece of wood that is freshly cut from the end-grain of a softwood or by carefully sanding the hardwood of tropical origin to get a clean end-grain. It is also important to select the most appropriate magnifier one that is 8-15x magnification. It is important to know what you're looking for e.g. in terms of the shape, pattern spacing, or colors.

Woodworking JOINERY TYPES

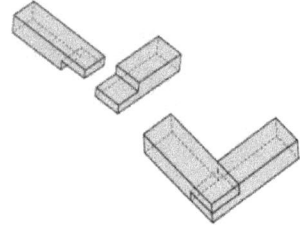

The term "wood joint" refers to the place where two pieces of wood come together and it could be as easy as a single piece of wood positioned on top of another or a number of interlocking slots. The joints are typically joined by an external force e.g. staples, glue, nails or screws. Wood joinery is an essential component of woodworking. Due to the diversity of types, you'll have several different joints to choose from based on the type of project you will be working on.

When you are able to learn the most popular wood joinery principles, then your woodworking skills will become effortless. Many people don't realize that regardless of whether you wish to master carpentry at home for a fun hobby or you'd like to make a living from it, understanding the different types of joints that are required to complete your project is essential. Because there are a variety of joint types that are alike with regard to strength or application, learning several methods gives you the widest range of options to select from. Some of the most commonly used and important kinds of joints are described below:

Basic butt joint

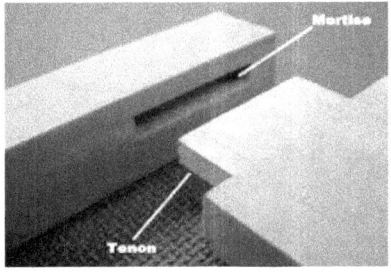

It is a kind of joinery in which two pieces are joined by just joining them. It is the most straightforward joint because it is a matter of cutting the pieces of wood to a suitable length and then join them. It's not the most sturdy joint, but can be extremely useful in certain situations.

Mitered butt joint

Mitered butt joints are similar to the standard butt joint however there is a difference that in the mitered butt joints, wooden pieces are joined in an angle. It's more attractive because it does not display any grain at the end. However, it is not the strongest.

Half lap joint

This is the point where an notch in each of the two pieces of wood that will be joined is taken away to allow the two pieces to are joined as a single piece. It is thought to be more durable than the butt joint , but not as strong since it could reduce the strength and durability of two adjacent boards. It is thought as ideal for different types of furniture where two pieces of wood will be joined in the middle, not at the edges.

Mortise and Tenon joint

It is regarded as an ancient ways for joining wooden pieces. It is the process of having a board put into a different one. This mortise actually is a rectangular hole that has been curved to the sides of a board. The Tenon is a piece that protrudes at the bottom of a second piece of board. The tenon fits snugly to the mortise, and extends out to the opposite edge of the mortised surface.

Tongue and groove connection

This kind of wood joint is the strongest, offering the adjoining surfaces which are essential in the process of preparing to join the joint. If you've ever laid a floating flooring or laminate, then you are acquainted with the joint tongue and groove. It is a method of holding 2 boards on their edges, and not the ends or at their centers. The edge of one board is bent out into the groove. The joining edge is then extended into a tongue that is supposed to fit into the groove. The tongues and grooves are slightly curved to allow the tongue to be able to enter it at an angle.

Dado joint

The dado joint is an ordinary joint that is used in woodworking. It involves a notch cut into one of the boards to allow the other board to fit. This type of joint connects the edge or the end of one board with the center of the other.

Dovetail joint

It is among the most sought-after and stunning joints employed in furniture and cabinet making. Dovetail joints are extremely sturdy joint and relies on the use of glue and a bit of skill to hold it in place. It also is not dependent on nail or fasteners. When making a dovetail joints, first make notches on the ends of two boards. The notches should be well designed to enable them to join as tight as feasible.

Rabbet joint

This kind of joint is called one called a dado. It cuts along one edges of a piece of wood and not in the center. It is employed to join cabinets or for making boxes in which two edges must be joined together extremely tightly.

Biscuit Joint

It is a practical modern joint. It is a technique where boards are joined at the edges using slots cut as well as using wood water to keep them in place.

Pocket joint

It's a kind of wood joint that requires drilling a pilot hole before cutting an angle-cut slot which should be in between two boards prior to connecting the two using screws. It is used to create frame frames for cabinets.

Chapter 3: Woodworking Basics

Woodworking is a fun pastime however before you start creating things with wood it is important to understand the fundamentals of it. This chapter will provide the basics you should to be aware of about woodworking.

Hand Tools to help Woodworking

Hand tools are extremely important for anyone who is woodworking. Hand tools are tools and equipment that aren't operated by electric power (power instruments). Here are the various kinds of hand tools you must have in your workspace for woodworking.

Claw Hammer

A claw hammer can be used to drive nails onto wood. Make sure you choose a hammer that isn't too heavy, and that feels comfortable when you hold it.

Layout Square

A layout square lets you draw a square line to mark the cutting of an ending. It also lets you draw an angle as much as 45°. If you're starting out with woodworking, select an 6-" grid square.

Measurement Retractable Tape

Tape measures enable you to measure precisely and accurately. A good tape measure will be marked with metric and standard marks. The retractable tape measure comes with locking mechanisms and loose hooks so that you can secure the measurements securely.

Utility Knife

The utility knife a multi-faceted cutting tool that can be utilized to mark a line on the wood. It is also a tool to scrub mortises on hinges.

Chisels

Chisels are essential hand tools for woodworkers. They are used to eliminate waste from joints and mortises. They can be employed to chip off additional pieces of wood that must be taken away. You must keep at least one of 1/4 " 1/4 ", 1/2 " 1/2 " in width and one" length.

Level

A level is an excellent instrument to find out whether a piece of wood is vertical or horizontal. You can utilize the long level if you're working on large woodworking projects , while a shorter 6" torpedo-level is perfect for small-scale projects.

Screwdrivers

Screwdrivers are similar to claw hammers, and aren't just for woodworking but also in other industries too. Have a variety of screwdrivers like the flathead type, the square head, and star screw.

Sliding Bevel

A sliding bevel is comparable like a layout-square however it is adjustable to any angle you desire. It also has the ability to lock, which lets you duplicate the angle you require.

Nail Sets

Nail sets are small , round tools that put the nail head under the surface of wood. This keeps the finish of the wood clean.

Block Plane

Block planes are used to cut thin pieces of wood out of the stock. It's great for making edges clean after assembly of the piece.

Power Tools to Woodworking

If you're just beginning with woodworking, you must learn how to work with hand tools. As you gain knowledge and experience you'll need power tools to develop more extravagant projects. There are a variety of power tools can be purchased to begin working with wood, but we will only cover the fundamental tools you will need to tackle various types of projects.

Circular Saw

This multi-functional power tool has a clamp-one edge which can also be used as table saw. It is able to cut fiberboard or plywood. If you're on a budget, be sure that the first tool you buy is the circular saw. They are available in a variety of sizes. However, when selecting a top circular saw it is essential to purchase one with high capacity to cut through the various kinds of wood you'd like. It must also include extra features, such as an anti-locking mechanism that permits the blades to slide if they get stuck to the stock, and blade locks that lock the blade spindle to the stock which allows you to change the blades with ease.

Power Drills

Power drills permit you to make multiple holes in the surface of wood. When purchasing a power drill, you should make sure that it has a an action that can be reversed and a the ability to hold them comfortably. It is also possible to select those which have hammering capabilities which can be useful when work on projects that are not connected to woodworking. Power drills come in various sizes, and the sizes are connected with the chuck. You should have the sizes 3/8-inch and 1/2-inch to ensure that you can drill different sizes of holes in the wood, if required.

Jigsaw

Jigsaws allow you to create curved cuts on boards of thin or plywood. A good jigsaw has a variable speeds and an orbital action.A Jigsaw that has orbital action lets the blade be slightly angled forward towards the material, which decreases wear and tear of the blade to ensure a more smooth cuts. If you're working with wood often it is essential to purchase a jigsaw with a cord because they're very efficient in comparison to cordless models.

Orbital Sander

An orbital sander enables users to smooth out the surfaces of wood with ease, rather than using sandpaper. When you purchase an orbital sander you should to purchase one with dust collector bags or filter to ensure that dust is not blown around. It should also feel at ease in your hand. Although sanders can vibrate, the best ones shouldn't jiggle excessively, which could cause fatigue when working on huge projects for sanding. Another advantage of a good orbital sanders is the adjustable speed control.

Compound Miter Saw

The compound miter saw can be great for cutting compound angles at the edges of the stock.A well-constructed compound miter saw is able to be adjusted 45 degrees or more towards the left or the right.

Woodworking Tools

When investing in hand power tools and tools is essential, it is essential for hobbyists as well to purchase quality tools for woodworking. Accessories for woodworking aren't just helpful, but they are essential in helping you complete the woodworking tasks you have planned. Here are the tools are essential for being successful at woodworking.

Woodworker's Bench

The most useful item you can have at your workstation is the work bench. It is made of solid, thick hardwood with a series of holes specifically designed to hold benches and a vise that can hold the item in place while you work.

Portable Shop Table

The great thing about working is that you will never have enough table tops in your workshop.This table is not heavy but durable and is equipped with retractable casters. It lets you tackle smaller projects. It is also able to be used in conjunction with the bench for workers for those working with big projects.

Tool Storage

There's nothing more irritating than having to search for your tools when you're in the middle of your work. Tool storage will allow you to organize your items. You can construct an organizer cabinet, drawers or build shelving to keep your tools. It is essential to keep your workshop tidy and tidy to avoid accident.

Clamps

Clamps are often regarded as the woodworker's most trusted friend.Clamps such as pipes, vise and bars help to ensure that your woodworking tools are stable when you cut or screw them to the floor.

Dust Collectors

Clean up your workshop by investing in dust collection devices like vacuums. Although most power tools come with ports that connect to vacuums but hand tools don't.If you're just beginning your journey using a vacuum cleaner, it can be utilized, however when you get more advanced in your pursuit You may want to look into a more advanced kind that collects dust.

Bench Grinder

Bench grinders are extremely helpful to keep your tools constantly sharp. They are a very affordable accessory that you can purchase for your workshop for woodworking.

Featherboards

Featherboards are used to keep the stock in relation to the edge of cutting of a router or table saw blade. This type of device lets you create intricate cuts along the edges of your board.

Chapter 4: Woodworking Strategies

How to square rough cut Lumber using the Table Saw

If you purchase rough cut lumber, or mill yourself your own wood, then you have to learn what to do to get them squared. Here's how to square them using the table saw. You'll first need to build a jig.

You'll need:

8 1/2" 8 1/2" x 48" small hardboard (if you intend to make many boards that are more than about 6 feet. long, you should use at least 96" long hardboard, and 1x3 below.)

1x3x48 inch strip of wood

Three toggle clamps

Measuring tape

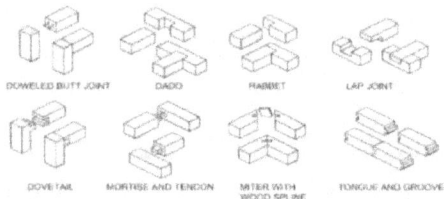

1) Put glue over one edge of the 1x3-sized board. place it in line with the long edge the wood (smooth edge down) and secure them until they dry.

2) Attach these toggle clamps on the top of the 1x3 to ensure they can secure a wooden board onto the.

3) Place the rough cut lumber on the jig, so you have one rough edge is facing towards the board. Then clamp it down, and measure the smallest spot on the 1x3 to determine the. Make sure you set your table saw to take off the bark of across the whole board.

4) Run the board, then jig across the blade using the 1x3 positioned to the fence.

5) Remove this board off the jig and then measure the tiniest portion of the board but this time with the straight edge that is now out. Make sure your fence is set correctly and run the board over.

6) You are now left with a squared piece of wood and you can use it with the miter saw to ensure an accurate cut.

How do I Edge Band Plywood

If you are planning to build shelves, Murphy beds or anything else made of veneered plywood You will need to be aware of which edges to be finished prior to when you can assemble them. It is only needed for edges that will be visible and you are able to mock put it together without fasteners in order to identify the edges that need to be completed. When you are sure of which parts require banding, put the pieces aside.

You'll require:

Edge banding that is pre-glued (one that is correlated with the species of wood that is veneered onto the plywood)

Edge of Single or Double Veneer Trimmer

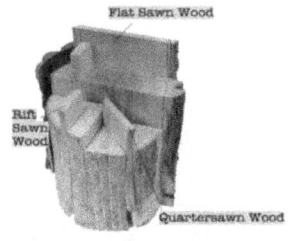

An iron

Small, smooth piece of wood

Scissors

Bench Clamp

Sanding block (120 grit paper)

1)Cut some banding a few inches greater than the edge that it's placed on.

2)Place the panel into a bench clamp that is fixed with the edges facing upwards.

3)With an iron on one side and a veneer strip of the opposite and begin to iron the strip on the edge. The heat warms the glue, which then adheres onto the edges. Be sure to be careful and stay steady the glue may be able to melt and adhere, but it will remain warm for a couple of minutes and is easily removed or moved. In the event that it does happen, just re-heat the glue, then cut the banding off and begin by putting on a new piece.

4)Once the entire banding strip is placed on the edge of the block, grab it quickly of wood and then press the glue between the banding and the plywood. The bond will be sealed securely. If you require longer boards, run the block of wood using the iron to warm the glue.

5) Let the glue set as you trim the ends of the strip so that they are flush to the edges of the plywood using scissors.

6) Next Take your double or single veneer edge cutter and drag it across each side of your board. Trim off any excess banding.

7) The banding must be exactly the same size of the edge it's been glued to, however it may be a bit rough. Use your sanding block to apply 120 grit sandpaper, and gently sand the edges, making sure there are no cutting and splinters. If there's any glue residue that has spilled out into the wood you should try to remove it as much as you can. This is a crucial step, especially if you're planning to stain this project. The glue will stop stain from getting soaked into the wood, and it can look shabby.

8) If there are multiple edges on the same board band, just rotate the board, then start from scratch.

Crosscutting and. Ripping on the Table Saw

When you cut boards using table saws it is because you push them into the blade, and the grain pattern and blade are going in the same way. They are also parallel. It makes any effort for pushing the boards through less difficult since there isn't resistance. Crosscutting a piece of wood on a table saw indicates that you push the board through the saw however, it is parallel towards the saw. Most of the time, you're cutting boards or pieces of plywood that are too large to cut on a miter saw. In most cases, having another person assist cut the crosscut is the most effective method to use. One person can hold the board in place against the fence and keep the other end hanging from the machine, while the other is pushing the board through the blade in a uniform fashion.

Quick Overview of the Different Types of Joinery

Joinery is the way to tell how to tell the difference between professional woodworker and one who is a DIY-er. Some methods are simpler than others, and certain are more artistic and others more functional. An excellent method to master to make traditional joints is called using the Lock Joint. It's a great method of making drawers as they're able to hold their shape during movements.

You'll need:

2 3/4" large scraps of thick material (having two boards of different colors is ideal since they are easy to distinguish in the process of learning)

Table Saw that comes with an Dado blade set at 1/4" thick, and a regular wood blade

1) Set your tablesaw with the 1/8" large dado. Lift the blade 1/8" up and keep it 1/4" to the side of the fence.

2) Crosscut one of the boards with the same setting. This is considered to be the drawer's side.

3) Set the blade's height at 3/8" tall. For the 'drawer front' position the second board up vertically in such a way that the bottom of the board is moved by the blade.

4) Next step, swap the dado that was set for normal blades, then adjust the blade's height to three-quarters" tall. Move the fence about 1/2" away from the edge from the edge of the blade (instead of the typical within the blade). Lay the 'drawer ' front down and then place the cut end against the fence, then push it through.

5) Combine your boards until you've got an Lock Joint.

Other types of joinery that are common are as follows:

An Overview of how to identify the Different Species of Wood

Here's a look at the various kinds of wood. There are many others, but these are the most commonly used for woodworking. Look closely to the pattern of grain, distinct colors, knots and other distinctive characteristics of these examples. Remember that the samples come with some coats of clear finishes on the surface. Raw lumber is generally more damaged.

Note the differences in White Maple, Curly Maple as well as The Birdseye Maple. These aren't distinct kinds of trees. In fact, they're all Maple however certain environmental conditions have caused them to have these distinctive as well as sought-after results. Around one percent of Maple logs are good enough to warrant being labeled Birdseye or Curly.

These patterns are more evident with the manner in which you deal with the log. The most affordable cut, the flat sawn, requires the least wasted work. The miller slices the log into slabs that are flat and will not see any distinctive markings within the grain. The quarter sawn wood has an attractive appearance however. In this case, the lumber is cut by cutting the middle out. Rift sawn is the least expensive method to buy. The miller slices the logs similar to the spokes on bicycle wheels, starting beginning in the angle (between 35 to 65 degrees) towards the outside. It is rare to find rift sawn woods in stock.

at the mill for lumber, however you can also request at the lumber mill.

Pine as well as oak, birch poplar, cedar and cherry. Hickory, cedar, mahogany and walnut are the most common kinds of wood you will find in nearly every woodworking or lumber shop. Other woods on this table can be more expensive and usually require special orders.

They're more expensive, however they're also more durable. Begin by working with the domestic lumbers until you master your craft before you decide to make the move to spend the money on exotic lumbers you need for your project. You'll be pleased by the final product, and you'll have a lower chance of damaging an item and having to purchase more. If you do fail to make the right choice, particularly with exotic woods be sure to keep it in the wood as you will be able to create something else from it, like cutting boards or knife handles carvings, or wood mosaics.

Chapter 5: Woodworking Fail-Free Skills, Tips and Techniques

When you begin to play around on woodwork, you're likely to make a few mistakes and create some work pieces that look unattractive. It's aspect of the process, and shouldn't detract from your work. Some people are scared of this, thinking that it's expensive making mistakes. If you have the right tools and a few tricks and tips to begin woodworking, you can get started and see your dream come to life without having to make the investment.

Essential skills and techniques for woodworking all woodworkers should be aware of

Drilling holes

It is a fundamental technique in almost all woodwork projects. A cordless drill can make it simpler for beginners however, as you progress in your abilities, you must be able to drill holes with other types of drills.

Painting

This is the ability that gives your project a professional appearance. It is important to choose the best paint to apply to a specific project. The most effective choices you can make are today's latex paint as well as oil based paint. It is also important to decide the amount of sheen you wish you want to choose, which can range from matte to gloss.

Sanding

This ability will allow you create an ideal end to every project you design to highlight the beauty inherent in the wood. There are various kinds of sanders to select from based on the task you're working on. You have the option of choosing between hand, orbital , or belt sanders. Sandpaper is available in a variety of grades, so the type you use will be contingent on the task.

Making the right choice of screws

Screws are always helpful to connect two pieces of material which forms the base of any woodworking project. There are various kinds of screws available in the present, and the selection of the screw you choose will be based on your specific project.

With the appropriate skills at the ready, you will have to tackle some projects to learn techniques that can take you further. Remember that you can't learn everything at once It takes time to get you to become a master woodworker. The amount of time needed is determined by the level of enthusiasm you have to master. The more you do and learn, the more you will improve and that means you'll be able to take on many more tasks as you improve your abilities.

Tips to help you get started Woodworking

Don't always rely on tape measures. They are essential, but make sure to cut the pieces in a way that is suitable. Always test the already cut pieces to verify that they fit perfectly. If you find pencil marks on a piece you measured previously it, you could always remove it to make it more comfortable.

Use only sharp tools. Tools that are blunt cause chips and tear-outs and can be a source of frustration for woodworkers. They can cause injuries as well. Sharp tools always function quickly, and with less effort, so risk of injury is minimal. You will get a neat cut at the end of the day which saves you your time as well as effort finishing sanding when the job is completed. You can learn sharpen your tools in order to ensure they remain in tip-top shape at all times.

Everyone who works with wood even the most skilled one, will make mistakes. If you make a mistake, acknowledge the error Learn from it, and move on. Do not dwell on the mistake since it could drag your confidence to a low. Make a plan to be better in your next endeavor.

Consider woodworking as a pastime so that it is enjoyable and relaxing. In this way, you'll be able to take pleasure in every moment of it. This is how you can create the top projects as a novice and make the transition to professional woodwork

It is possible to seek assistance. There is no need to be a solitary person trying to try to figure it out on your own. Woodworkers are always eager to assist one another and you can learn a lot from a fellow woodworker. Join a woodworkers' forum to discover, exchange ideas, and increase the confidence of one another.

Chapter 6: Woodworking Tools

Power tools are a bit overwhelming and even dangerous for those who are just beginning their journey. It is a maze of tools, and so many types of each one that it's difficult to do your homework. This article is an outline for anyone who is interested in woodwork or woodworking tools. We will cover drills as well as saws, routers, and sanders.

Drills: This kind of tool offers a wide range of tools by itself however, many of them can be left out to use for woodworking. The majority of boxes, such as combination drills as well as SDS tools have hammering motions used in woodworking, but they are not necessary and could therefore be ignored. If you're looking for an item in the near future, you can purchase an item with hammer action however, if you have an excess or are just looking to work with wood, other alternatives are available. The best tool to use for wood work is a flat box an revolving box, or a motorized box that is cableless. They can be employed both as a boiler as well as a screwdriver. both a hammer and screwdriver are available and these tools are usually functioning both forward and reverse.

Saws: There is many kinds of saws on the market, including circular saws, mitre table saws, and reciprocal saws. Each is different and has their strengths as well as weaknesses. Jigsaws are perfect for cutting curves circular saws are ideal for portability when straight cutting mitre saws are great for creating lengthy pieces of lumber with bevel (angle) table saws are great for cutting large pieces of big pieces of lumber or reciprocal ones (also known as saws) are great for cutting raw material and general demolition.

Tools for planning: These tools can be used to level out wood surfaces. Hand planners with power are great for small spaces, while larger parts-planing machines are more efficient. Planer thicknesses are also feasible- the features of thickness are similar to a planner, which guarantees that the board is kept at one point and the other in a similar length. The operator is able to perform regular workpiece movements, and each moment a tiny amount of pressure is applied to lower the cutting machine until it is at the level of the entire body.

Routers: A routing device functions similar to the hammer, in that it creates holes in wood surfaces. Routers can be used to make holes that do not touch the surface of the wood, and the round holes may expand into lines of long length. A router can create esthetic enhancements to edges of surfaces, such as bookcases, desks, and desktops with specific attachments.

Sanders Sanders: These are crucial tools for those who love woodworking because they can be used to improve the appearance of the wood for instance, in anticipation of the application or as component of the process of finishing. There are various kinds of sanders: belts are great for the removal of heavy stock or dimensional sanders, orbital sanders are finishing sanders that combine random orbit sanders with an upper surface removal speed as well as delta sanders. They come with an pointing sanding pad that can be used to sand tiny areas into corners.

They are essential woodworking tools and you could require at least two of them to complete any project. While working with electric tools the safety of workers should be a top priority. This is why we advise wearing gloves, safety boots and glasses.

Staub extraction must also be thought of. This is usually integrated into tools like circular saws, which produce an enormous amount of dust and you can purchase special tools for dust removal from the best woodworkers, such as Festool.

What are your top woodworking tools?

There is a certain one if you own many pieces of equipment within your workshop. Do you have a modem the plunge saw or a set of chisels? It is recommended to use for the one that is cord-free. In the kitchen cordless drills are an absolute requirement. My cordless drills work great and also funny since they have quick release attachments.

*Keyless Chuck

*Eccentric Chuck

*Shift to release screws tip to holder.

This material makes it easy to maneuver into small space.

Another of my most used tools for woodworking is my carpenter's biscuit. I'm able to join anything. It's perfect to join Miters since I can achieve a an elegant and smooth joining during the clamping and glueing process because of an angle-sensing stop that can be adjusted.

My most used hand device is my block plane, and it's a smaller variant of the No.4 hand plane . It fits into your in your palm. It's great for small tasks like mouldings, and is it is easy to put inside the top of my toolbox.

My wife must tear me off from the section of tools every when we visit the store for hardware. My collection of tools for woodworking could be three times larger in the event that I were not married. It's a shame they're too expensive. I'm a sucker for woodworking tools. There are some extremely cheap manufacturers however the quality tools are not suitable for industrial applications. I've tried cheap equipment, such as the angle grinder and sander and quickly realized they were not of the same quality. equipment isn't as good as that of well-known companies. I spent just $15 for these machines, so they aren't comparable to a $90 tool. If you're on a limited funds or perhaps just every once or twice is something you're looking to use the tools, then these less expensive versions might be the best choice for you.

A wide range of woodworking tools is available. The table saw is a must. The table saw is huge in its size. This kind of saw has an elongated shape for the blade. In order to explain in detail, it's an aluminum disk that is circular in shape or blade, and it has its edges teeth. It also has the machine that rotates or runs the leaf.

The benefits of this circular sheet is that it has a small blade is able to slice it, has a tough surface finish, is able to make precisely straight cuts, and typically produces burrs and needs to be made geometrically to allow this type of blade arrangement. In table saws, this type or circular saw blades can be employed. There are four primary divisions of tables. They're like this.

Table saws for benchtops Table saws that are hybrid, table saws for cabinets. Benchtop table saws. In comparison to table saws in general that are top-of-the-line, table saws are the cheapest and less efficient. In certain situations they are able to provide enough flexibility and precision. The motor used by the benchtop isn't very secure, as it utilizes just traditional generators. However, these engines are more efficient in regards to weight and size.

When you look at the table used by Contractor, one could observe how the table is larger and the weight is more heavy. A build-up of dust in this type is a little difficult. But, for those who are prepared to make use of the product at home will find it the best for them. It uses the engine to provide induction.

Cabinet saw is contained inside a cabinet that houses an electric motor. The cabinet is mounted Trunnion. Three v-belts of the same design are used for this. There are many advantages to using it. Even though it is quite it is heavy, vibrations are decreased and the durability enhanced. Dust accumulation is made possible by the massive cabinet that it occupies. In comparison to traditional saws hybrid saws are comparatively low in cost. They offer the same benefits to traditional saws like cabinet saws.

The product also comes with a case to ensure the proper storage of pollen. It is now part of the products that is available. Some table saws ' accessories are feeding or routing tables feeding fence, rip planks, hold down, fence mitre crosscutting, sledge gages insert, tenon jig and stacked splitters as well as dials.

Woodworking tools: Selecting the best tool for the task

A perfect tool and equipment make up a large component of woodwork. To create a great piece of woodwork, talent and skill aren't enough. You require the proper type of tools and equipment to shape your ideas to become catalysts.

Chisel is for woodworkers of all kinds the most common and indispensable of hand tools. Chisel is a great tool for cutting edges from various tough materials like stones, metal, or wood. When you purchase a chisel two aspects should be considered in the fitting of the handle chisel as well as the quality of steel. The majority of woodcarvers and craftsmen utilize blue steel for Japanese chisels specifically. It is possible to choose handles made of boxwood like the octagon-shaped shape. For a better grip. Make sure the steel is cleaned and sharpened. Any specialist will help you to avoid injuries.

If you are planning to purchase squares, be aware that the words used for squares are precise and exact since they are the guidelines in any woodworking strategy. It's a great deal at less than 0,003 cm. If you are comfortable, you are able to purchase just 3-4 inch squares.

There are a variety of saws employed in woodworking and their roles vary for each one. When it comes to any home renovation project the trim saw that is on the opposite part of the blade generally employed to repair jobs.

The only thing you need is a unique style I'm sure. But you'll need the right equipment and tools to realize your dream design. Don't think of these tools just as machines, but they're more than just that. Take excellent care of them. Make sure to sharpen, check and regularly polish them regularly. This will not only give you the best value for your money, but can also help prevent accidents when performing your most favorite tasks earlier in your life.

The best woodworking tools can be compared to a kitchen knife in terms of their use. The constant use of these tools results in wear and tear that could render them ineffective and decrease their effectiveness. A dull saw takes longer to cut a piece wood. In the same way, it is an extremely difficult task to employ a slower drill bit when compared to a sharp drill bit.

The primary thing to remember is that high-quality woodworking equipment must be maintained in a clean and well-formed. It is vital to make sure that all the tools you use for woodworking are properly maintained. It is possible to find as numerous strategies and methods of sharpening and grind as the various kinds of equipment for woodworking are readily available. The equipment is also a crucial factor in determining the shape and method of sharpening. It's also a matter of your personal preference.

The following tools are among the most frequently used tools to sharpen or grind stones.

The tools for grinding and sharpening are the best. This technique helps sharpen the sharpness of knives, scissors blades, as well as other woodworking tools. Stones come in varieties of sizes and shapes. They typically are made from human-made or carved stone. They are not self-powered and are categorized into different grades by the size of the particles of the stone. The size of the grate's size is directly related to the effectiveness of the finishing of grinding and sharpening. It guarantees that the larger grains, the smoother the final result of sharpening. But, this also means that the finest grains are made up of less material. rougher ones. They can also require more time to allow the grinding and sharpening process to complete. The most common sources of this kind of sharpening and moulding equipment are whetstonesas well as oilstones. Japanese water stones.

Files are utilized to form and smooth the surface of a material. Files are tools equipped with a thin, parallel ridge that covers rough steel bars. Files are an instrument used by hand and is ideal for grinding and sharpening instruments, like cloves, saws, and chisels.

Bench Grinder Bench grinder is a device used for the creation of smooth surfaces. It can serve as a buffer, polisher or sharpening tool according to the kind of wheel used inside the engine.

They are a popular fixture in woodworking shops. They are quick multi-purpose, flexible sharpeners. They are able to be used to sharpen and sand automobiles. This is the best instrument to grind and sharpen. They're quick, accurate, and user-friendly. They are easy to use and do not have problems.

Apart from the above that are widely used grinding and sharpening tools, there are numerous other options available. However, these techniques are often used for multiple uses. The finest woodworking tools should be properly maintained and maintained regularly. This indicates that your work is rewarded with a spectacular result. It will help to keep your position and efficiency.

How to Purchase Cheap Woodworking Tools and Equipment? Tools

It is only necessary to have basic woodworking tools if you begin a new woodworking activity. Woodworking professionals of every stage must work with routers and drills, grinders, lathes, sanders as well as woodworking tools which are expensive. Unfortunately, you cannot solely use one tool and you'll have to purchase a number of them in order to create the layouts you'd like to see them. If you begin now, it is important to seek out machines that are less expensive, so you don't spend too much.

When you find a reliable supplier of tools, this offers you the most effective options for finding your device from a range of choices. You can also compare several items this way and locate the one you require.

Check first your local hardware stores and shops. This is a great way to start If you do find what you want it's simple to buy it at any time you require it. It is possible to check prices online prior to visiting an hardware store. You can also look for stores with discounts so that you can reduce costs and save time.

If you're familiar online shopping, eBay is a great location to search for equipment. eBay is full of amazing deals; however, you do not know what the quality of the tools are since professional woodworkers do not sell their equipment, instead you purchase the tools from websites such as eBay. It is also unclear if they're a reliable vendor to purchase from. If you do find someone you buy online, stay with the person, and don't arbitrarily purchase from another person. This will save you a lot of money , and you can be sure that you won't be scammed or be smacked off.

Check out the yard and garage sales section of your local paper for bargains on specific appliances that you can use. It doesn't mean that it's not worth buying however, ensure that you discover it is utilized by someone else in your field , before you make a decision to purchase it.

The majority of wooden stores will offer various kinds of tools and equipment that are available for sale. You might want to you should look at their website for discounts and deals.

Where can you purchase your basic woodworking equipment and machinery for cheap:

If you start in woodworking, you'll eventually require general woodworking equipment to assist you in your craft. Every type of woodworker uses lathes and routers, as well as grinders, factories, and sanders. And everyone who works with timber knows the price of producing timber. It is not possible to use just one tool and you must put money into a few of them to get the most out of your woodworking.

If you decide to continue, however it is now time to locate equipment that is less expensive to ensure you do not pay for too much. A reliable source of equipment and machinery can offer you the best options to choose your equipment with a variety of options. It is easy to compare parts and pick the one that you prefer.

Local retailers and many department stores are the best places to search for equipment. The nearest DIY hardware store is a good place to begin, as you'll often locate the right equipment and then face it, it's easy when you're looking for something.

Many of the woodworking resellers are likely to have a wide range of tools and equipment for sale. You may want look through their websites for deals or even free shipping. We typically have a wider selection of items which you won't find anywhere else. Be sure to check over the Better Business Bureau and see the legitimacy of the online seller to ensure that the money won't be redirected to you.

Auction websites like eBay are great sites to get great deals. The only thing I've seen is that you don't be aware of how reliable these devices are since heavy woodworkers will not offer them for sale. Also, you don't know how reliable sellers on the internet are as you aren't able to check out other's actual feedback. The thing I've learned is that when you locate an online auction site that specializes in less expensive equipment, and you find it reliable adhere to the source and avoid another. It is always a good idea to keep an excellent source in the long-term since it could make a huge difference in your savings.

Who can purchase used tools? It's a great idea to saving money by purchasing used tools for woodworking However, it's essential not to buy your first set of tools. There are many sellers on the website and also meet other vendors when you begin shopping at flea markets. However, it is important to remember that certain tools used for woodworking could be a waste of money instead of a wise investment.

There is a huge difference between the tools that you require if you are working as an trader in the woodworking trade as well as the tools you will need when you are working as an individual hobby. If you're an artist and you are considering this as a job and you are a professional, you must be extra cautious. It isn't feasible to purchase expensive tools that aren't used for woodworking projects. Therefore, only shops which sell used products for professionals should purchase your used equipment for woodworking. It will allow you to meet your expectations and acquire what you need and desire. Everyone will be happy with the offer as they'll save money as well as generate profit.

What old tools can I purchase? Maybe you are wondering what old tools could be bought without wasting money on useless equipment. It doesn't matter as certain equipment and computers can be repaired. It's a sign that engines can be fixed and make an old machine the same as a new one. It's not a good option to purchase the original engine that was left in an old machine. It's going to be a waste of money away, and that isn't something you'd like to do.

Find second-hand woodworking equipment that will be affordable for you. However, don't just look at the dimensions, but consistency is, in the end, the most important factor which is why you need to focus on.

Thickness Planner - Knowing This Amazing Woodworking Tool. What exactly is this?

The thickness planer is an electric powered device that cleans wood into small, incremental layers. It allows users to cut wood to precise sizes which are necessary for high-quality wood, like creating cabinets or furniture.

What is the process?

The typical thickness floor comprises the rotating cutting head with a few removable dual-sided blades. The blades spin at high RPM, which flattens the sides, and then cut the wood to the required size.

The majority of best bench spacers for portable connect to an ordinary wall outlet (120v) and the motor is not just for the blades, but also the feed rollers. Typically, they run 16-26 feet of speed. The input roller typically has straps that push timber into the floorplaner, and the output is usually fluid, so that there are there are no marks left on the final plates.

The blade's head is able to move upwards and downwards to alter the thickness you require. A majority of them have depth gauges However, depending on the machine the accuracy varies.

What are the signs to look out for?

The majority of these machines measure 12-13 "long and 7 inches in height. They seem to weigh a lot when it comes to compact devices are in the field. They can range from 60-90 pounds. Or so. Because the motor is responsible for equally the feeding roller as well as the blades, it is likely that you'll need to choose a motor in the range of 2-3 HP.

Chapter 7: Simple Diy Woodworking Projects

Here are some useful and simple designs that you can build to construct basic furniture such as shelves or a stool.

DIY floating shelves

Shelves are simple to construct and are very useful, too. To get started Here are some incredible DIY shelf ideas that you can make:

This is a straightforward and practical woodworking project can be completed in just about an hour or so.

To accomplish this, you'll require:

Clamps

Screwdriver or drill

Screws

two pieces made of 1/4 inch 2 feet x 4 feet of sanded plywood

Two pieces 1" each two inches by 8 feet. pine board

Stud finder

Level

Paint brush

Painter's tape that has Edge

Paint or varnish

Directions:

Step 1

Cut the pieces of wood below into the dimensions listed below. To determine the exact size, you should seek help from the staff at any hardware or depot shop you visit to purchase the materials.

4 - 1-in. 2-in. 21-in.

8 - 1-in. 2 in. 6 1/2 in.

4 - 1/4 -in. 8-in. 21-in.

4 - 1/4 -in. 2 inches. 8-in.

2 - 1/4 -in. 2-in. 2 inches x 21 3/8 inches.

Step 2

Join these pieces of wood to form your frame. The frame should appear like this:

Step 3.

Apply glue, nail or fix the sanded boards on the framework. Connect the shelf to the frame by using a screw driver. After that, screw at least one stud finder in order to secure it.

Step 4

When you're sure your shelf has been level Add the remaining screws. After that, you can attach the second shelf. Be sure to use identical measurements.

Step 5

Attach the 1-inch 2 inches boards on the sides of the shelves. The rest of the 1/4-inch boards onto the sides. When the glue is dry you can coat the shelves with paint.

This is a fun project and is very simple to complete. The shelves can be placed in your bathroom, bedroom or even in your living room.

DIY Honeycomb Shelves

Honeycomb shelves are pleasant to look at and can put anything you want on them: figurines, books, scented candles, as well as porcelain decors.

To create an individual honeycomb shelf you'll require:

Miter saw

Wood screws

Drill

Drill bit

Level

Rotary sander

Tape measures

Wall brackets

Wood glue

3 Fencing planks

Marker

Directions:

Step 1

Make sure you set up your saw miter to cut the planks in a 30-degree angle. After making one cut flip the plank on its side and take a measurement of the long ledge. You must ensure that the long edge is 12 inches. You should mark the location in which you'll make the next cut. After that, you can make the second cut. Then, you will have the initial piece to make your honeycomb shelves.

Step 2

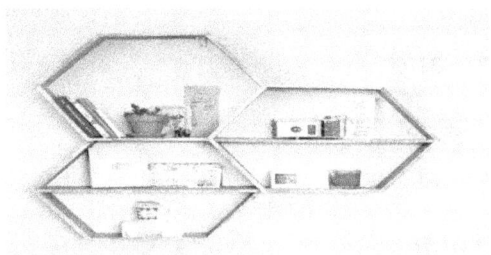

Repeat the procedure. You'll need to cut 15 12 inch pieces. Be sure that all pieces are the same dimensions.

Step 3.

For one hexagonal pod, select six pieces of wood and place them in the middle of your floor. Connect them to form the shape of a hexagon. You'll feel as if you're joining to a puzzle. Utilize a wood club to join the pieces. The sides should be pressed tightly.

Step 4

With a drill or a drill you can pre-drill the holes before you decide to connect two hexagons. This will make it simpler to screw and it stops the wood from breaking, too.

Step 5

Repetition steps 3 and 4, until finished by making the first hexagon. Repeat the process until you've created three hexagons connected. The honeycomb shelf should appear like the following:

Step 6

To hang your shelves locate the studs, then attach your brackets to them. Install the bottom portion on the bracket, first. then apply pressure on that bracket on top. Be sure it's sturdy and can support some weight.

Step 7

Place your shelves onto the bracket. After that, you can indicate where you'll put the next bracket. Place the brackets you'll need to reinforce. Now, you're done!

The honeycomb shelf is fun appealing, beautiful, and easy to build. This is an activity you can make with your family and friends, or even your children.

Leather Strap Shelf

This is a stunning and fashionable shelf that will bring a sense of style to any space.

Materials:

Screw gun

Staple gun

One inch leather strap

1x6 inch of plywood

Paint (Any color can be used)

Directions:

Step 1

Paint the plywood, and allow it to dry for a couple of minutes.

Step 2

Join the two ends of the leather strap of 1 inch to each other. Fold the ends in two ways. Then, secure the strap's ends onto the wall by using the screw gun.

Step 3.

The painted plywood should be slipped into the leather strap. The strap must be at least 3 inches away from the shelf's edge. Request someone else to hold the second strap and then slip the other end of the wood into the other loop of ribbon.

Step 4

Make use of a level to make sure your shelf's straightness. After that, attach the second strap to the wall with the screw gun. The straps should be secured under the plywood with staple guns.

Be aware that the shelf can only hold small objects, so make sure to avoid placing things that are heavy and breakable on it.

Woodwork Plans for a Basic Bookshelf

This woodwork design is great for people who are new to woodworking. It doesn't require many equipment to finish this. This project is extremely simple to accomplish, it might be your first woodworking project.

Materials:

Router

Electric drill

Power sander

Cut off the saw

Two pieces 1 12x1 and 3/4 of 1 inch thick pine wood

4 pieces of 1 11 x 3/8 of an inch of pine

1 . Piece of x 4 pieces of wood

Table saw

Clamps

Carpenter's square

Deck screw

4D finish nails

Tape measures

Wood glue

Screw gun

Screws

3/4 " nail to secure the back

Directions:

Step 1

Sand the pieces of wood to enhance the texture.

Step 2

The bigger pieces (1 12) are the upright. Therefore, you will need to cut a small dado or slot. It should be at least 3/4 wide with a depth of 1/4. This will allow for the smaller shelf boards.to be able to climb into the wood, and then be joined to the larger wood.

Step 3.

Cut the dadoes in two across the boards with the router. It is also possible to make this cut using the table saw if do not have an router.

Step 4

The dadoes can be sanded again using an electric sander. Once the wood has been cleaned, put the shelves together with wood glue. Put the glue on the top of dadoes in order to provide the shelves additional durability. After that, place the boards in the slots for dados. Begin by placing one end on the shelf and move the shelf around. Make use of a hammer to fix the shelf in the slots of dado. Make sure you clamp it tight enough so that the glue can be set. Make sure to clamp it for a night.

Step 5

Remove the clamp. It may be necessary to add some reinforcement in the clamp, so screw in screws to the sides with an screw gun.

Step 6

Then, place the back of the shelf. Cut it in accordance to the width and length of your shelf. You can then attach it to the shelf. If you wish to decorate your shelves.

Simple Workbench

If woodworking is something you'd like to do then you must have an adequate work bench. Here's a bench can be built in less than a day. You'll need a few basic tools for this.

Materials

2x2s to frame the frame and legs

2 x4 lumber to make the frame

1/4" plywood that could be used as a top for a workbench

Circular saw

Bar clamps

Chisel

Square

Hand drill

Screws

Wood glue

Step 1

The legs should be cut. The length should be 78 centimeters. Make use of a measuring tape as well as pen to draw the length of wood.

Step 2

The next step is to cut the pieces to join the legs. Cut four 2x4 pieces that are about 55 centimeters in length. Then, put the frame together by nailing and screwing the pieces to each other.

Step 3.

Then, drill the edges of the frame and join the legs. After that, insert the screws into the previously-drilled holes.

Step 4

Then, attach the rails onto the legs. It's much easier when the bench is lying on its back.

Step 5

Cut the plywood to match the dimensions that the frame will need. After that, you can screw to the to the top of the bench onto the bottom.

Done! This workstation only costs around $15! Consider all the money you'll save by making an item of furniture from scratch.

Three-Legged Stool

Materials

Pine log

Screws

Power Sander or Sand Paper

Varnish

Band saw

Planer

Three aspen logs

Knife

3 aspen logs

Hammer

Nails

Directions

Step 1

Make a cut from the log with the chainsaw

Step 2

Cut the wood to about 2 inches in thickness.

Step 3.

Make a circle with the wood. Cut out the circle with an a band saw

Step 4

Then, smooth the surface with a planer. Cut three 14 inch aspen logs. These will be the legs for your stool.

Step 5

Cut the aspen logs with an instrument. Then then, smooth them.

Step 6

Attach the legs to the wooden logs with an Hammer. Then paint the stool with varnish. Allow it to dry.

Now, you've got yourself the option of a stool! You can build as many stool as you want.

Simple Chair

This is a basic 2-x4 chair design that you can build within a couple of hours.

Dimensions

17 1/2 " 18 1/2" 37 1/4 "

Materials

2 pieces of 2x4s that are 10 feet long

One piece, 8 foot long of 2x4

Drill

Saw

2 1/2 " screws

4" screws

Wood filler

Wood glue

Paint

Sander

Cut List

A Two pieces, 37. 3/4 to make back legs

A - four pieces in 10 1/2 " for front and back boards

C two pieces 16 1/2" to make front leg

D two pieces out of 15" side boards

E - 1 piece 13 1/2 "

F Three pieces in 18 1/2 " to make the seat

G Two pieces from 17" in length for seat sides

Directions

Step 1: Make the back.

It is the first thing to do to construct your chair's back. You will need to gather two back legs as well as the three back and front boards.Then build them according to the diagram below. Join the back and front boards with the legs with the 2 1/2 screws as well as a Kreg Jig. You could also make use of wood glue.

Step 2: Put together the front.

When you've built the back, you will need to put together the front using the front legs as well as the back piece as seen in the image below:

Step 3: assemble the chair.

Make use of the sideboard pieces to join the back and front sections. Attach these pieces to the front and back sections of the chair with the screw gun. Take the following illustration to guide you:

Step 4 Step 4: Make sure to add the supporting.

Install thirteen and a half " long length at the rear of the opening for the seat. This will provide the seat boards a bit of area to rest on.

Step 5: Put the seat in place.

Join the seat with screw and wood glue. Follow the instructions below.

Step 6: Done.

Sand the chair, and then apply paint.

Porch Table

This table is simple to build. It can be placed on your deck and in your kitchen. It can also be used to serve as a study table for your child.

Materials:

Three pieces of 20 inch fence posts to support the tabletop

Four pieces from 1 1/2-foot posts

Four pieces of wood to make the frame

Screw gun or drill

Screws

Directions:

Step 1

The frame is assembled with the screw. After that, attach tablestop pieces into the frame. It should look as follows.

Step 2

Place your leg post in an X-position and connect the two posts by screwing them together in the middle. After that, you can attach each X leg onto the outer edge of your tabletop.

Voila, you're done!

The Frame Wine Rack

Wine racks are simple to make. Therefore, it's a good idea to start with this task before making something more substantial like a table , or a bed.

This is a six-bottle holders that's easy to build. To make this happen you'll require:

Two pieces from 1" hinges

Two parts of" by 10.5" Birch plywood

Neon string is about 12 inches long

Screwdriver

Sand paper

Drilling with 1-1/" drill bit , and 3 1/2 " hole drill bits

Carpenter's square

Directions:

Step 1

Find out where the inside on each wine bottle cut out will be using a carpenter's square and pencil. Each wine bottle must be 12 inch in distance from one another. It should be like this:

Step 2

Cut six holes in each piece of wood, resulting in twelve holes.

Step 3.

Sand the plywood and put the hinges on the top of the rack. Install the hinge on one side and repeat with the other side.

Step 4

One inch is measured from the side and bottom of each piece of plywood. Drill an opening on all four sides of your rack.

Step 5

After that, you can loop the string through one of the holes , and tie it in place to secure. Then, loop it through the other hole. Make a knot, and then cut the string. Repeat this procedure on the opposite side.

Rustic Hairpin Drink Holder for Legs

This piece is ideal in the event that you own a restaurant due to its strong visual appeal. You can also put this piece in your home as well.

Materials:

Old Crate

Hole saw

Screw gun

Screws

2 Leg pins

Pencil or marker

Carpenter's square

Plywood approximately identical in dimensions to the size of the crate

Plywood

Directions:

Step 1

Utilizing a carpenter's square, or a ruler, mark marks in the center of the bottle to indicate where each one cut out must be placed. After that, drill 8 holes in each end of the container.

Step 2

Install the plywood in the open area of the crate.

Step 3.

Screw the hairpin legs onto the opposite side of the crate.

It's that simple!

Crate Shoe Display

If you're a fan of shoes it is likely that you desire to display your precious items. The most effective way to accomplish this is to design an exhibit of shoes in a crate.

Materials

Nails

Hammer

Sandpaper

6 Crates

Directions:

Step 1

Your display of crate shoes will look something like:

Therefore, you need to line up three crates, and then connect them by a side.

Step 2

Then, you can line up the remaining three crates and then nail them together to make another rack.

Step 3.

Then, you can nail the two racks to each other. Sand the shoe racks and paint it if you wish.

This shoe rack will cost you between $5-$10.

Dry the paint and then put the sign up in your living space.

This woodworking task will boost your creative skills. You can choose any color you wish. Also, you can write any humorous or inspirational message.

Chapter 8: Security Guidelines When Utilizing Tools

Woodworking with hand or power tools is an enjoyable activity, however, as with all tools one must be aware when working with woodworking tools , otherwise you run a the risk of accidents and injuries. There are common sense safety precautions to be aware of when working using tools. Do not get too convinced that "it will never occur to me" or be in a rush or in any hurry. It is essential to read the safety guide of the owner with guidelines for a safe working setting.

If you want to be successful in coming up with useful products that you can admire, you need to be sure of your personal safety. The machines are only useful if they are properly used. If you think that a specific instrument isn't maintained properly or you are concerned about its efficiency, do not going any further. First, gather some information that is satisfactory and then continue working on the project.

Put on the safety Equipment

The most important safety rule is to use safety equipment. Keep your hands protected from all scratches or bruises, by wearing gloves specifically designed for woodworkers. They also aid you when you're putting the the final touches to your wooden piece.

Surface planers, drills and routers produce a lot of sound that isn't appropriate for the human ear, especially in the case of work for a long period of time. Wear hearing protection. There are two types of hearing protection i.e the ear muffs as well as expanding ear plugs.

Wear safety glasses each when you begin working by hand or using power tools. Eyesight is extremely valuable to us, and you should not put it at risk at any cost.

Safety glasses of various kinds are available , but all share the same characteristics. Side screens are a great way to shield yourself from dust by with power tools or sawdust.

Masks and respirators for face are recommended while working on the router or on sanders. They can cause harm to the lung. It is recommended to wear a protective mask to prevent harmful particles from getting into your lung. Paint and varnish can be cause harm, so it's better to wear a respirator in order to ensure your safety.

Full face shields are available for complete face protection.

The right clothing

A comfortable outfit will allow you to perform your work more effortlessly. Be sure to stay away from loose clothing, scarves, tie and jewelry. If we are talking about the proper clothes, that means that your skin should be protected from the fluttering chips of wood.

Clothing that is loose can pose a risk since it could be stuck with any machine such as cutting blades or saws. Unintentional actions on your part could result in serious injuries. It is important to avoid wearing long sleeves too.

Do not remove your shoes when working by hand - or power tools. Avoid open-toed sandals and shoes. The shoes should be comfortable.

Get rid of the necklace, bracelet, or earrings prior to beginning to use the equipment. Jewelry that is hanging could pose a the risk of injury.

Avoid distractions

The world we live in is filled with distractions, and it is wise to avoid these distractions when working using equipment. Do not listen to radio while working, and try not to speak to anyone in the absence of shutting off the machine.

Children should not be allowed to enter the area in which you've begun working. They could hurt themselves or be troubled by their activities and curiosity.

Avoidance of Alcohol and Drugs

It is recommended not to work if using drugs that cause a the sedation effect. It is risky working with tools when under the effects of alcohol or drug. Make sure you are clean and avoid the urge to drink from a can in your wood area. Keep out of the room when you're not fit to do woodwork.

Woodworkers need a clean and safe area to work.

Beware of working in areas where there is a water or oil spills. It might not sound crucial, but ignoring this fact can lead to sliding. It is not intended to create fear, but to inform you. Clean up your workspace before leaving work with the help of a brush. You want a tidy space to return for the next day.

Weather conditions that are suitable

Don't work in the event that your hands or clothing are damp or if a tools got wet during rain. Avoid working in rough weather conditions like rain or storms. Don't use electric equipment while standing in water.

Disconnection of power to electric tools

I've heard of unfortunate events, such as woodworkers losing fingers due to lack of care in cutting off the electricity from a tool. This is an easy guideline to follow to ensure your security. Always turn off the electric power when you have to replace the blades or the other vital component of the device.

Sharp blades are used for cutting

Be sure that all bits, drills, and blades are in good condition and that the blades have been sharpened. If the saw blade isn't sharp, you'll have to work harder to achieve the result. It could exhaust you. Be sure to keep your tools in top state. If you detect an unnatural odors or see smoke, stop work immediately and look for any malfunctions in the machine.

Save the leftovers or cut-off material to use in an alternative creative project.

The right lighting conditions are required.

It is vital to be vigilant about your eyesight. It is essential to be aware of the right lighting when working with tools or sharp blades. The dim light can hinder your vision, and the finished product could be full of flaws. You will only be able to be able to read measurements with precision or draw lines to get correct angles when you are working in a bright lighting.

Use single extension cord

Here's a great advice for woodworking safely. Make sure you use just one power cord on all power tools 110V. This way, you'll have to turn off one device before plugging it into another. It can become a habit of disconnecting the power before making any adjustments on your tool.

Other measures to protect yourself

Store the wood in a dry area to keep it from getting damaged by tools.

Be careful not to reach for a tool when its blades are moving. Switch it off and wait for the blades to stop, then unplug the device to cut off power. Clean the cut-offs, or do whatever you're planning to. Also, don't move away from the machine while it's operating. Turn it off, then go out of the area.

It is essential to keep an extinguisher for fire within your reach in order to avoid a disastrous scenario.

Maintain the floor and surrounding tidy and keep the cords away from one another. The wires need to be moved either under or overhead to avoid cords getting caught.

Chapter 9: The Reasons to Should You Learn Woodworking?

Woodworking is a craft that has existed since the beginning of human civilization. The greatest aspect about this occupation is that you don't need to be doing it on a an all-time on a regular basis. You can perform it part-time and thus take part in other business activities.

Once you've learned to construct wooden objects and tools, you can make an amazing present for the special person within your own life. It is not necessary to purchase the most expensive gift to your spouse or acquaintance. You could create something unique for them and let them feel valued and loved.

It is also possible to use your woodworking abilities to make some cash by commercializing your idea. For instance, you could begin making furniture, and later sell it for profit. It is also possible to start making wood according to the specifications of the customer.

Make it a hobby. Woodworking is among the most enjoyable hobbies because it can keep you entertained and will help you turn your creativity to use. Additionally it's a low-cost and enjoyable pastime.

Are you aware that you can completely transform your house and enhance its aesthetic value by using wood products? It's all you have to do is know how to create wood items and you'll be good to go. You can, for instance, create a unique dining table that can completely change the interior of your home. It is also possible to build the perfect chopping board to impress your guests when they lay their eyes at it for the first time.

Researchers from around the globe estimate that it takes just 10 seconds for a person whom you've just met to get an initial impression of your. If you're considering expanding your business or bringing on more customers You must put an individual appearance in your workplace. For that, you need to create a unique and appealing piece of furniture, and put it on your desk. If a potential client walks into in your workplace, they'll get an impression of you, and consequently improve the likelihood of concluding an agreement. What is the kind of person who would not want to do business with an organized, unique and tidy person? Furniture will show you as an extremely well-organized, focused and tidy person.

Are you thinking about having a exclusive piece of furniture? something that you can't find anywhere else. To stand out from your fellow colleagues and peers You can choose to create something with wood. You could, for instance, make an effigy from yourself and your animal.

What should you do if you purchase an 42-inch television, while the largest wall unit on the market can be used with the size of a 24 inch television? Don't worry. You can always construct the wall unit if have the ability to do it. If you have woodworking abilities, you can construct something that's not accessible in the market.

The purchase of furniture that is high-quality is expensive and could cost you money. Although you'll need less time to build, it's less expensive to build than purchasing furniture. Therefore, you should consider building instead of purchasing furniture.

If you are able to master woodworking and are proficient in woodworking, you will never need to hire carpenters to fix damaged furniture. Repair the damaged furniture by replacing the broken piece or by repairing it.

There is no need to purchase plastic furniture if you are unable to get the cost of wooden furniture.Wooden furniture is attractive and can make a office or home appear more natural. Another drawback of plastic items is that they're not long-lasting. When you master how to work with wood, you are able to make furniture for your office or home.

Your woodworking skills can bring you joy and increase your self-esteem. It will feel great by being able to point out the furniture piece within your home and tell the person who visits that you're the person who made it.

Chapter 10: Woodworking Projects You Can Master At Home

At this point, you're likely looking forward to getting started However, you're probably thinking about what you can learn at this point. The good news is that there are plenty of tasks you can do at home, even if do not have a lot of experience.

It is important to note that you will require extra equipment for the following tasks, so make sure you know the items you will need before beginning.

Storage Box

This project will require you to spend a day on it and will enable you create something useful.

What you'll require:

A miter saw

Hand sander

Drill

Glue, Pencil, Screws

2 hinges and pins, Clamps, Set square, Ratchet straps

Jointer for biscuits and number 10 biscuits. You'll need to cut around 20 biscuit joints.

19mm x 144mm soft wood to make a box of 800mm x 800mm x 800mm x millimeters (L,W,H)

Step 1 Cut the wood to size, but make sure not to subtract the width of your piece from the length of the box to ensure you can get the proper size.

Step 2: Draw your lines so that you are able to determine where you will cut using an biscuit jointer.

Step 3: If you are using your biscuit joiner be sure the blade is located in the middle of the biscuit. Also, make sure that your blade is in the middle of the biscuit as well. Utilize the pencil markings as a reference and then cut an additional 5mm on the left and right side so that your joints are slightly wider. This can help if you don't meet the required mark.

Step 4: After you've made all of your joints, glue the two sides together without glue. This will let you know whether they are a good fit. If they do not fit you can make small changes until they fit.

The 5th step: Now is the time to apply the glue Make sure to apply the glue evenly. After you've added the glue and bonded the joints, wipe away any glue residue.

Step 6: Use your clamps to bring the wood together in a way that it is held in position. This will help ensure that you have the correct size lid and base.

Step 7 7. Now it's time to cut some support angles. the pieces of wood you cut will ensure that your box is supported more. Take measurements of the corners of the box from top to bottom Then, make use of 2x2 timbers to cut those angles. Sand the edges. Then, you can glue the supports to the box, and then add screws, if you like.

Step 8: Remove the biscuit joints and join them with the lid pieces. You can add a few more biscuits to make the joints more secure.

Step 9: Set the lid and base on the box , and using the jigsaw, finish the box's corners. If you'd like to create shapes or molds using a router, you can accomplish this.

Cutting Board

This project is quite enjoyable since it utilizes scrap wood. There may not be a lot of scrap wood in your yard at the moment however that doesn't mean that you can't go out and purchase some. Scrap wood is generally affordable, and there's no problem with it. the wood is just leftovers from other projects. The ideal choice is to choose wood that's already coated with varnish, but if not, you must apply varnish in a variety of shades and let it dry prior to using it.

Before you purchase any type of wood, you will need to determine how large you'd like your cutting boards to be. The size of boards can vary from 24 x 16 inches up to 28 x 24 inches.

You'll need:

Table saw

Planer

Jointer

Router table and router with round-over piece and round groove

Cauls

Clamps

Sander

Wood glue

Brushes

Step 1: Join and plan your wood if it's rough. Join an edge. Each piece of wood must end with a smooth edge and a smooth face , too.

Step 2: It's time to lay the wood in a straight line on your planeer, making sure that the pieces are smooth and smooth on both sides. This will ensure you have of the same in thickness. You can always use the initial piece of wood you planed and joined to serve as a reference. Ideally , your wood should be approximately 5/8 of an inch in thickness.

Step 3. Cut random widths of the wood so that your piece has more individuality. Be sure that each strip of wood is smaller than 1/2 inch thick. Variate your width board to create an attractive looking board.

Step 4: Once you've cut your strips, spread them out and arrange them in a way that they look nice. After you've decided on the layout you'll choose, you're ready to begin glueing. Set half of the wood on the left and the other half on the right. and then join the wood pile to the left and then glue the other wood to the right. Secure the wood with clamps, so that the wood is at the right position.

Step 5: Allow the glue to dry and then, if you wish, plane the two halves prior to joining them and securing the two halves in place using clamps.

Step 6: You'll have to sand the wood again, but this time you'll need to do it manually. After you've sanded your wood then cut the edges to ensure they're straight.

Step 7: Prior to you present your partner with the work you've done and then apply a finishing to the wood to ensure it is able to be utilized. Be sure to apply butcher's block oil or mineral oil. This will ensure the wood is protected and make sure it looks great regardless of how often it's utilized.

Chapter 11: What to Beware of/ Do's and Don'ts to Avoid When Choosing Wood

One thing that may confuse the novice woodworker is how to select the right lumber. Terminologies like board feet, quarter-sawn, rift-sawn, etc. can be confusing for novices. But, these concepts are easy for a professional to remember. In this chapter, we'll review the basics for a beginner, such as you could visit your local mill or lumber yard and select lumber without looking like an idiot.

Softwood or Hardwood

The first thing to think about before visiting the local mill is the kind of work you're working on and whether you'll be using softwood or hardwood. Hardwood's strength is measured through an Janka tests for hardness. It involves placing an iron ball on the surface of the wood, and then compressing it to measure the distance as well as how many pounds requires for the ball to penetrate the wood. Wide oak is a lot harder to soft pine. It is generally more expensive than Softwood and you have to choose based on the type of instrument you're creating. For example, when making the case of a violin, it is made up of both hard maple and soft Spruce to create different resonances in music. Another example is a bench that could have a top made of hard maple, and an underside of soft yellow pine. This is based on what you intend to use it for and how well you'd like it to withstand the abuse.

Flat-sawn vs. Rift-sawn vs. Quarter-sawn

Another thing you may want to think about when selecting lumber can be the grain's shape. The grain structure is what determines the strength of the wood. Unless you're looking for exquisitely figured wood to make a front-facing panel, you'll require something more durable. Lumber companies usually employ something that is called "through-and-through" cutting, wherein they'll take a log and just slice it downward.

In this, you can find different kinds of cuts. The flat-sawn cut is one of them. When you cut a flat-sawn piece the grain is curving semi-circularly that is extremely unstable. This is a more economical method to make lumber, however it isn't well for furniture due to it's tendency to be a cup or twist. It's one of the issues you need to look for regardless of whether the lumber is twisting or cupping. Another kind of cut typically will be the cut that is quarter sawn. The easiest way to tell if the board is quarter-sawn, or not is if they have an incline that is vertical. The higher that the vertical grain runs, the more solid this board is which is ideal for furniture.

Another cut type is the one that is rift-sawn. Rift-sawn boards are usually inclined at around 30-60 degrees. However, for quarter-sawn, the standard of 60 to 90 deg. Rift-sawn boards have 30-60 degrees angle grains that are quite stable, as it produces extremely straight grains on the top on the surface of the wood. This is interesting in the way that it provides the board with a modern appearance.

Another method of obtaining sturdy wood is by the process known as Riving. Riving involves splitting wood using a hand using of a wedge an axe and mallet. The wood is generally damp, and has a moisture level over 30% during you are riving. Rived wood has perfectly vertical grains , which makes it extremely stable. For woodworkers, except for a source of wood that you can work with on by yourself, quarter-sawn is the most ideal option for any job. Be aware that the majority of mills do not have the entire amount of wood they have set aside to be quarter-sawn. One good way to do this is to carry a razor-sharp block plane with you to the mill and then use it to reveal the end grain if it is difficult to see it, in order to make sure it's got that beautiful vertical grain. This is the most important thing to consider for solid furniture.

Wood Defects

Wood imperfections are an important issue to watch out in the wood you are evaluating to be used in an upcoming project. Wood defects can include knots that are extremely difficult to remove using the hand plane, and wormholesthat allow you to look inside a sap wood. It is generally recommended to stay clear of sapwood, or be prepared to cut it out. Be looking for signs of cracks or splits running through the grain at the end. There's as well twisting and "wind" across the timber, and this can be a big problem for any wood work. There are a myriad of issues that can go incorrect with it, therefore examine the sides and ensure there's no twisting as it's going to take many hours to flatten it. Pick the top boards that you can and avoid these issues if you can.

Where can you purchase your Lumber?

Another issue that could be on your mind is where to purchase the lumber you need. Local mills that offer reasonable prices are generally more affordable. There's a wide range of wood to choose from and generally, the guys are fun to work with. However, if you don't own an existing mill in your area then you can look for a wood dealer. They carry a large variety of wood, and some offer mail-to-order options as well. The option of mail to order is generally not recommended however, it all depends on the credibility of the hardwood dealer, as it's usually a good idea to examine the wood prior to buying. If you are in a city, you might prefer to find woodcrafts in the vicinity. Woodcrafts are an excellent alternative, but they don't offer much volume, so their prices are usually slightly more expensive. If you're in the city and there aren't any alternatives nearby and you're looking for a bargain, then this is a good option.

In Quarters, Board Thickness

When you're a woodworker looking for wood at the lumber yard, it is important to be aware of how to talk about the thickness of your board. In the lumber industry , they make use of "quarters". For quarters, an inch of wood is four quarters; 4/4 = 1". Six quarters would be 1 inch thick. 6/4=1.5". Eight quarters equals two inches, 8/4 = 2" and the list goes on and on. Keep these in mind to ensure that you don't be unable to communicate with the man at the mill.

Calculating the Board Feet

Then, you'll be required to understand how to calculate the number of board feet. The board feet calculation is how lumber dealers calculate the amount they'll charge you for lumber. You need to take an instrument with a tape and measure how thick the boards are in inches. Then, multiply it by the length of the boards in inches. then multiply it by your board's length in inches. Then divide it by the number 144. You will get feet for the board. You can multiply it by the cost your local mill charges per board foot.

The thickness of the feet on the board is (inches) (inches) x Width (inches) + Length (inches)

144

The majority of hardwoods will come with more expensive prices than softwoods. It will be helpful to estimate the price you'll spend before you make the purchase.

Wood Moisture

The last aspect to be taken into consideration is the wood's moisture. If you plan to visit your local mill, it's recommended to carry an instrument for measuring wood moisture. Don't buy the cheapest moisture gauge choose one that has received positive reviews, if it is possible. There have been many disagreements among woodworkers regarding the amount of moisture a piece of wood must have to be before it is in a position to work with it. The consensus among woodworkers who are experts on and has been the norm for a long time is that if you put the moisture gauge into the wood and you find at least 22% of moisture that the wood shouldn't require sitting in your shop for an extended period of time before you begin working on it. However when the moisture exceeds 22%, it's a great idea to allow the wood to adjust a bit and sit within your shop for some time. Be sure to place small spaces between each board to let the moisture be able to escape. If you're riving timber from your personal wood supply it is best to leave it within your workshop until humidity drops to an acceptable level.

Chapter 12: The Small Furniture (Beginners Plan)

1. Bathroom Shelf Unit

Tools and Materials:

2- 3/4 6 1/2 X 32 side Lumber

1-1/2 9 1/2 18 Top Rail

1-1/2 5 1/2 inches x 18 inches Top Shelf

2-1/2 5 1/4 inches 18 inches mid and bottom Shelves

1-1/2 7 18 Bottom Rail

1- 5/8 diam. 18 Towel Bar

No. 8 x 1 1/2 wood screws

Steps:

STEP 1:

Once the boards are taken to their length, you can mark the angles for the side pieces. With the sketch on the page facing you as a guideline You can trace the outline directly on one board , and then cut it out with a saw (if you feel confident). An easier and more secure approach is to draw the design on a piece of cardboard, then cut it out until you are certain it is a good fit and then trace it on the board.

After cutting out one piece of the side, use it as a reference in drawing the contour onto the opposite side piece (or make use of the cardboard pattern and flip it over). This will ensure that the two pieces will have exactly the identical curves.

Then draw the wavy lines for the 18"-long sides of the top and bottom rails. To create symmetry in your design, grab the 9" wide piece of cardboard or paper then draw an arc over it. Cut the design out and then trace it onto the first half of the 18"-long piece. Flip the board over to trace your design on the second half of the card. Repeat the procedure for the bottom border using an alternative curve (as illustrated in the sketch).

When you're dragging your jigsaw along the curves, steer the blade in a smooth manner so that you don't cause bumps or bumps that you'll need get rid of later. A lot of jigsaws come with an adjustment dial that lets you to alter the blade's stroke to be either soft or abrasive, based on the type of wood you're cutting (and your mood).

STEP 2:

Then Cut off the crescent moon onto the sides of the pieces. (If you'd like to skip this extra feature.) Draw the shape in the place you'd like it (making sure that it's not exactly in the same location that the rail at the top or highest shelf) and then drill a large hole through between the two moons. Put your jigsaw blade in the hole and cut the moon. You must definitely utilize the scrolling blade to accomplish this. Scrolling blades tend to be much more delicate than a normal jigsaw and is able to handle edges that would cause the standard blade break.

Step 3:

Once you've cut away the pieces, you can round around the sharp edges using sandpaper. It is also possible to employ a cornering tool to soften all straight edges. An Veritas cornering tool does a quick work of smoothing out the edges of pine (see the image). If the tool's blade breaks or is a bit slack it, you're with the grain. Consider pulling it away from the opposite side of your board. The grain lines will tend to curve in the direction of knots therefore you might have to switch directions many instances, yet it's quicker than sanding.

Step 4:

It's tempting to put the entire unit together now however there are a number of advantages to placing your stain or paint or clear-coat over the pieces individually before going any further. It's much less difficult than having to paint every surface of the shelf after it's put together. In addition, the glue squeeze-outs will adhere to the wood surface during the assembly process. However, when your boards already have an exterior coat it is possible for the glue to be removed.

The image here is finished using shellac. Shellac must be applied using a gentle steady hand, in even long strokes that don't cross (see picture above). Since it's alcohol-based it is extremely quick to dry which means there's minimal time to wait. In the event that you're making your own Shellac using a solvent that's good, you should use one that you can purchase from a trusted woodworking supplier.

Even if you do not work with shellac for your final option You can apply some quick dab of shellac over knots. It will seal knots and keep sap from leaking into the finish you've chosen. Shellac is an excellent primer coat for almost every finish, with the exception of stain.

STEP 5:

Now it's time to "dry install" the entire unit. Lay it out with the shelves, sides and borders in place. Secure everything with a light clamp then square up the shelving with the speed square. Make sure that the clamps are strong and sturdy. Make use of a pencil to draw an outline of the sides under each shelf for to refer to later on when doing the final assembly under the stress of being aware that glue is just beginning to set.

Step 6:

Once all clamps are in place, drill pilot holes for the screws to avoid splitting shelves as you are driving the screws. After that, on the top of the predrilled holes for screws you can drill deeper holes to an approximate thickness of about 3/8" in order to create a hole for the plugs which will cover the screws' heads. To prevent drilling the plug holes too deeply it's recommended of wrapping a bit masking tape over your drill bit, 3/8 inches from the tip so that you know when to stop (see the image below).).

Step 7:

The next step is the "wet fitting." Remove each piece off and place a tiny amount of glue around edge of shelves as well as the borders as well as a dab at the end of the towel bars. Assemble and secure everything and then drive the screws. Make use of a moist cloth to clean any glue that is leaking from the joints.

To create plugs to cover the screw heads you could use a plug cutter bit. It is a tool that can be inserted into your drill as a normal bit. It cuts tiny circular wood plugs that disguise the heads of the screw, so the final product looks neat.

After your screws are set Once you have your screws in place, start the plug-cutter and slice plugs from a pieces of pine (see the photo). After you've cut approximately thirty plugs. Use the screwdriver or knife to remove each plug of the hole it was placed in.

Instead of cutting your plugs yourself, you could purchase pre-cut hardwood plugs from the hardware retailer. This is probably more convenient, but there are several disadvantages. The hue of the wood won't match, and it's not like pine in terms of absorbency,. Therefore, the plugs react differently to finishes and won't blend with the rest of the decor.

Step 8:

Before inserting each plug into the hole, make sure to place a small amount of glue on the inside of each plug, and spread it around.

Once you have the unit pluggedin, wait 20 seconds for your glue form. After that, use a flush-cutsaw for cutting each of the plugs in line with the cabinet's surface. cabinet. If you don't own the ability to cut flush then you can cut the plugs out quickly by using a sander stuffed with sandpaper 80-grit. After the plugs have been cut and sanded, you can touch the plugs and the sides of your unit using shellac or the finish you're applying.

It's now time to put your wall unit. One method of mounting is to attach two 2" pieces of plumber's adhesive (which is prepunched with holes) to the side of your shelf. then elevate the unit onto waiting nails that are anchored into studs that are above the toilet. The studs you choose to anchor are an important thing to do as you don't want your cabinet to fall over on you at a crucial moment.

2.Handy Box

This toolbox is great to store all the everyday tools you'll use in at home--a tackhammer, tape ruler, screwdrivers, additional screws and nails and more.

The methods employed to construct the box are easy and enjoyable. Miter joints employed here require the use of a table saw for cutting every 45deg angle (a circular saw could also be employed, but it will be more challenging). Because of the huge space of the beveled joints the glue bond is enough to create a solid connection in this case.

Clear finish was utilized in the project shown to make the wood clear. It is possible to finish this project -- and the other ones--how you want using stain, paint or whatever you think will best suit your preferences.

Materials and Tools

2-1/2 6 16 Plywood Top as well as Bottom

2-1/2 7 1/2 x 16 Plywood Front as well as Back

23 3/4 x 6 7 1/2" Plywood End

1-continuous hinge (3/16 inches) x 1/2 ") x 16 ");

1 draw bolt

1 screen door handle

Steps:

STEP 1:

Cut the pieces according to the dimensions on the Material List. After that, tilt the tablesaw blade until it is 45 degrees and then attach the sacrificial fence onto the fence of the saw. Adjust the setting until you are able to cut a 45deg bevel along the outside of the box pieces. This configuration lets you cut bevels on pieces that have had their size cut this is more convenient as compared to trying cutting all of the parts to the right size and bevel them all at the simultaneously.

A note of caution Note: Take care when handling and cutting plywood after cutting bevels across the edges. Plywood edges are brittle and easily damaged or chipped. Additionally, you may get painful cut marks from these edges due to the fact that they're sharp.

STEP 2:

Double-check the 45deg bevel in order to make sure a perfect 90deg angle is created. This is crucial for the components to join in a straight line when glue is applied.

Step 3:

Draw out the bottom A The front and back B as well as the ends of C are laid out in a horizontal fashion in the manner illustrated. Apply the clear tape used to secure the joints to create an edging. Make sure that your bevels' sharp edges join as neatly as you can when you tape them.

Step 4:

The whole thing upside down, and then use glue all edges that will come together when folded.

Step 4

STEP 5:

You'll need some clamps to secure the joints in place. Be careful not to apply too much pressure, since it will cause the joint to distort and open it upwards at those sharp points.

Step 6:

After the glue has dried take the clamps off then place glue over the edges of the beveled edges and then secure the top.

Step 7:

Make use of blocks beneath the clamps to equalize the pressure. You may be thinking that you can attach the top of the entire assembly once all components are flat in the third step. Yes, you can!

Step 8:

After the glue has dried after drying, gently scrape off any glue squeezing. Remove the lid from the box with a table saw.

STEP 9:

The lid will be perfectly inside the box when using this method.

STEP 10:

Take a measurement of your hinge's thickness hinge. The table saw's fence should be set according to the measurement and cut an through-cut.

STEP 11:

Set the fence back to the size of the leaf on the hinge (this is not that barrel on the back of the hinge) and then make the clean cut. The cut will square off the corners of the rabbet.

Step 12:

Installation of the hinge. If the cut is precise the hinge will line up with ease by putting one edge of leaf against the rabbet's shoulder. If you allow that the roller of the hinge extend past the edges of the container, it is possible to open the lid. is able to be opened in a 180 degree angle.

STEP 13:

It's a simple but tidy and neat way to set up the hinge. It is now time to put in the draw bolt and handle for your screen door.

STEP 14:

After you've completed the box the corners will be the appearance of a neat, tidy look. It's a sturdy connection. The surface of the glue is huge There are no splines or biscuits are required.

Chapter 13: You must Have Personal Safety Gear

The personal safety equipment that are listed below could be a great help in protecting you from the most dangerous situations during your work. The mere possession of safety equipment is not enough. All safety equipment should be used in a way that protects your from injury.

The need for certain products might not be obvious however the dangers are extremely real. Very few woodworkers require being aware of the force of a rotating saw blade or cutterhead for jointers.

Unknown are the long-term consequences of exposure to the noise generated from power equipment. We've also provided the length of time for which an unprotected individual could be exposed to different levels before they risk permanently losing their hearing.

Remember, as well, that even brief exposure to noise although it might not cause hearing loss, it can make the senses dull and reduce an alertness in a woodworker to spot a setting to avoid an incident.

Safety goggles

Flexible, plastic eyewear protects eyes.

Vent holes perforated protects against injury from impact and sawdust. Type with baffled vents shields you from chemical splashes. Non-ventilated goggles are also available.

Face shield

The clear plastic shield shields you from splashes and flying debris Head gear can be adjusted.

Rubber gloves

Handles for use at home or disposable gloves guard against the effects of mild chemicals or finishes Neoprene rubber gloves protect the skin from caustic finish products.

Ear muffs

The muffs are cushioned with an adjustable plastic headbands protect ears from the high-intensity sound of power tools.

Work gloves

To handle rough lumber usually, it is equipped with gloves made of leather or thick fabric and fingers with knitted or elasticized wrists.

Safety glasses

Standard plastic frames that come with shatterproof lenses shield eyeballs from falling wood chip and other debris. usually, the frames come with side shields.

Dual cartridge respirator

It helps to reduce the risk of breathing in fumes while working with chemicals or spraying an finish.

Chemical cartridges and interchangeable filters provide protection against certain dangers and prevents the inhalation of dust.

Cartridges purify air and remove toxic substances through an exhalation valve.

The earplugs come with a neckband

The detachable foam plugs are compressed and then placed into Ear canals protect from noises from power tools that are high-intensity Neckbands made of plastic fit around neck.

Reusable dust mask

It has a neoprene rubber frame or soft plastic frame, with an adjustable strap for the head and the possibility of replacing it with gauze filter that protects against mist and dust.

Disposable dust mask

It can be worn over the mouth and nose to provide protection against the inhalation of dust or mist. It comes with the option of a fiber or cotton shield that has an adjustable headband and an adjustable nose clip made of metal.

A 1/2 horsepower drill press will not cause hearing damage unless you use the machine for a long period of time. exposed to noise generated by the 1 1/2 horsepower router could cause harm after only 30 minutes. Remember that equipment that have dull blades or cutters create more noise than those equipped with sharp cutting edges.

How do you test the air inhaler for leaks

A respirator can be as effective as the seal it has to your skin.

No seal, no protection.

In order to test the respirator's effectiveness, you must place it on your faceand place the strap that is the highest over the top of your head.

Adjust the straps to the sides to ensure a perfect fit.

For testing the respiratory device, close the valve on the outlet by your hands and then breathe out slowly.

There should not be any air leakage in the facepiece.

If there is air leakage from the respirator, adjust the straps to ensure a better fit.

Replace the face piece if required, following the instructions of the manufacturer or change the respirator.

Make sure you use the correct filters for the task in hand.

If you're sporting a beard you should wear a full face mask that has forced-air ventilation.

Chapter 14: Simple Woodworking Projects To Start With

Beginning students should begin by working on simple projects that require a basic amount of expertise. There are plenty of free blueprints for download that can be found on the internet. Some examples include simple wood equipment, birdseeders, or other decorative items.

Below are some of the most popular tasks that beginners can get started with:

Loveseat Glider Rocker

Making an entire chair from scratch is a breeze particularly for chairs that require uniform, straight cuts. A love seat glider rocker is a good example although it is time-consuming requires no advanced level of expertise to make. Making the chair takes about 30-40 hours, and the final details (e.g. smoothing lines, levelling etc.) can take between 20 and 30 hours.

The loveseat can have a redwood stain, or it could be painted using poplar. The choice is completely dependent on the woodworker's visionary ideas.

Bird Feeder

This could turn into an attractive bird habitat within the backyard. There are a myriad of ways to design an output. For beginners, it is possible to start with a simple but attractive output made of plexiglass with edges as well as a top that could be opened and a sufficient-sized perch.

Wind Chimes

One of the least expensive and most simple tasks to tackle is wind chimes. You can make them using small bamboos carefully molded with power tools. Because this is a simple project to create, parents with kids could let their children be part of the process, and help with a few simple and secure tasks.

Louvered Window Shutters

Louvers are apertures with slats that permit smoke or air to flow through but also block sunlight or rain from getting into the space. They are not just beautiful, but they're excellent for creating privacy to a space or even in the home. A lot of woodworkers are hesitant to think they're a bit sloppy and difficult to create but in actual they're quite easy to make. The key to getting the desired appearance is using the correct router Jig.

The entire project takes about 6 hours to complete.

Planter Boxes

A different and attractive project you can work on is an ornamental planter box. The name suggests that they are designed to house diverse kinds of greenery within the home or outside on patios - depending on what you like. There are numerous methods to design these easy outputs. Ideally there should be an drainage system at the bottom that allows any excess water be drawn away.

Making a planter container takes 6 to 8 hours, based on the size of the container to be constructed.

Chapter 15: Engraving

Not all cuts or scratches on wood are worthless, however some of them enhance their value. The process of engraving involves the carving of images or writing on wood. The art of engraving began centuries ago, as people made use of sharp tools to identify important events or to communicate information to a vast number of people. The mid-19th century was when the craft became popular as a leisure sport. It became more boring during the 20th century, with the introduction the motorized tool.

Beginning wood engraving means getting yourself some of the following tools:

Wood

Scorper

Spitsticker

Burnisher

Ink, rollers and glass

Sandbag

Stones for sharpening

In addition to these basic equipment, there's additional tools to create letters that could completely change the appearance of wood into a distinctive one. However, using these tools requires you to master specific skills for each one of them.

Chip carving - You can create divots using the use of a sharp chisel, by creating two lines that are angled across the middle. The letters' depth will depend on you, and every design you design is unique. By using gouges, you can form the letters by hand and then smooth them out or add precise punctuation or sharp point.

Dremel - Whirring tools can produce deeply-cut, sharp lines on the majority of wood species.

Lasers - With lasers engraving is now a distinct art form that is used in decorating homes and sculpture. It is a great option for small plaques that are used to signify the family's crest, individual accomplishments or simply write whatever you want on a piece of paper.

Wood burner - A pen-shaped wood burner allows the letters that are engraved onto the wood have a distinct shape and color. For those who are new to the field this device is user-friendly. The wood-burning pen makes it easier to do the task of an engraving tool. All you have to do is to put adequate pressure onto the pencil that it doesn't simply slide across the surface or scratch the wood.

The best woods for engraving

While you're eager to give engraving a go on your projects, make sure you know what kind of wood you're working with. This will help you decide what you should do, since different woods don't work for engraving.

The easiest type of wood to work with to make engravings is softwood. It's not easy for hardwoods to be burned. When engraving is complete, the shade produced is dependent on the hue of the base wood you select. Dark woods are able to hide the engraving, but lighter woods will create a dark, deep-burn that won't break easily but makes a distinct contrast in the style.

To determine if the wood is light or dark it is necessary to look at the content of the sap or resin. Woods with a high resin content will produce dark burn images. A few of them are Alder, Cherry, Mahogany, Walnut, Oak, Basswood and Ash.

Woods that have a low content of resin create images that are sluggish. A few of these are Fir, White Pine, Larch, Yew, Cedar, Redwood, and Spruce.

When carving letters with wood, a hand-held tool provides your letters with sharper edges and appear different from the designs made by hand-held devices of today.

If you look online, you'll come across many letters available to download. Remember that it is difficult to sketch the exact pattern you'd like to imprint on the wood when the letters are small. After you have drawn the design that you'd like to draw with the letter carving templates then engrave it on the wood.

Be sure to place your tool on the correct angle, otherwise you won't be able to see clearly even when you're using top-quality tools. Keep an angle of around 20-30 degrees to ensure that the tool you are using makes lines in the wood that aren't being able to run off.

Chapter 16: Woodworking with Pallets

Pallets are now popular. The common shipping crates were once discarded when shippers had finished using the crates, but recently it's been realized that they have a purpose that goes beyond shipping. In this chapter, we will look at the many possibilities to use your wood to work for you - using pallets!

Palletized Shoe Holder

The pallet is designed and made to function as an ideal shoe holder. It is fitted with slots where you can put your shoes. This is possibly the most simple pallet or woodworking task you'll ever have to commit to. All you have to do is purchase an ordinary pallet and finish sanding it. Some people might like the rustic look, however for this , smooth is the best option since you don't want rough sides of the pallet to tear into the material of the shoes you put in them.

However, using an instrument for wood joining or with a small piece of sandpaper, you'll be able to do doing your best to sand the pallet until it's completely smooth and uniform. Then, rub some varnish on the wood, to give it a beautiful shine and sheen.

Once you have established this, it is now possible to move the pallet towards an object or corner, and start inserting your shoes to the slots. Why not get your feet off the floor and take off your shoes and place them inside the Palletized Shoe Holder!

Patio Pallet Dog House

All you need to complete this pallet project DIY is two pallets that are standard in size and an item of cardboard. After you have your pallets, just put them on top of each other in the "A" shape, and then connect the pallets on top using screws made of wood. In order to make an additional backing for your dog's house put a nail or glue on it to the bottom of your structure. This will provide that muddy pet to rest their head during the next storm. Simply put this piece of wooden dog house in your yard and your dog is now ready to go into.

Pallet Bed

Pallet bed construction is an simple one to make by using just a small piece of pallet board. Just take a complete pallet board and pass through your jointer to smooth all rough edges. Once you've completed this, apply the wood finish on it to add a final edge.

The varnish on the wood will give your pallet the right amount of shine. For the sake of texture, let the board to dry for a few days. Then, you can lay your mattress and your other bedding on top and you'll have an instant bed made of pallets for you to sleep on!

Pallet Wine Rack

If you're an avid wine lover, you'll be awed by this simple diy. Start by acquiring an old pallet. Any pallet that has been left over from at a grocery store or warehouse can be used. Try to obtain permission before using it.

After you have purchased the pallet, you're going need a prybar and hammer for removing portions of the wooden pallet. Utilize the pry bar to take off the top half of the two-by-fours horizontally. Following this, you can use your electric saw and cut the lower half of the pallet away from the remainder part of the frame.

Now , you can grab one of the two fours that you've pried off before and cut the piece that is about 1 foot long. The piece can be put on top of the lower half you cut off. It will act as a bar to divide your wine rack on pallets.

Then, grab your power drill and make two holes in the back board of the rack. One at on the upper part of the rack and the other one at the bottom. All you need to do is connect it to your wall using wood-working screws. After you have installed your wine rack, you can now fill it with the wine you like.

Chapter 17: Tools Shop

The first thing a beginner woodworker should accomplish is to create an endurance race. As with the other tasks that woodworkers who are just beginning their careers must do, the foundation of a marathons helps to develop the skills and pleasure of the craft after the novice is becoming an expert woodworker. Storage options for tools are usually not adequate for the unique needs of hand instruments with their ease of use. The general lack of consideration about the unique requirements of hand instruments conspires to limit the capabilities of any potential hand instrument maker. In contrast to modern stores, where each new purchase of tools requires an additional flooring space after the necessary hand-tool functions are created, there's no need for additional expansion. The trick is to get the areas placed in this manner that they do not hinder your chances of succeeding.

Room to Plane

A workstation can be used to plan hand-to-hand as well as a variety of joinery procedures. You can't make extended passes of 8' over the inventory that rests on the size of a 6-foot seat. Cutting the inventory prior to moulding is not a good idea because it has disadvantages.

A scrap piece of scrap placed between your inventory and the wall can be used as a protection for the material being shaped. The walls also stop materials from being taken off the trunk and provides an ideal location to purchase the chisel rack as and other storage for instruments. A cushion that prevents fatigue in your chair is more than just a nice touch. Plane shavings can make flooring that is finished in concrete or wood. They can be very slippery, even if they've been swept away. The process of planning a large inventory involves some foot functionality and I would suggest a non-refundable, sweepable workout mat of some kind.

Space to Cut

Watching by hand gives woodworkers the opportunity to learn about the traditional joinery.Like everything else that attempts to learn how to watch, it is easier to observe great tools and the best space.In the stores of the Anglo-American cutting is performed with by sawhorses using the wide-bladed "western" saw. The dimensions and the shape are crucial to ensure that the ripping fits perfectly with the seat. I believe that this 4'x11 rectangular shape will be the minimum size for the best hand-tool store. One advantage of working with wood with hand tools would allow you to operate a huge inventory that is too heavy or difficult to be a muscle on machines. Being able to tear in the direct vicinity of your workstation will prevent you from having to bring several huge boards to your shop. However, if the there is a tight space it's possible to tear nearly everywhere. It's quite easy to get your sawhorses and tear the patio or in the backyard.

Anglo-American woodworkers escaped with tail vices for over 100 years and we will too. Don't leave any space at the top of your chair for the offcut. A long cut isn't easy to support in this case anyway.

Tool Storage Space

Employed tools aren't like hand-held instruments. In the event of their falling, it is typically fatal. Tools made of metal are much more susceptible to rust, which could result in pits appearing on shiny steel blades. Wooden instruments are prone to variations in humidity. Finding efficient ways to save hands-on tools is an efforts of skilled craftsmen for years. In contrast to proposing the most radical idea made from medium-density fiberboards, a quick review of what's been accomplished may prove to be a wise choice.

Photos of preindustrial stores clearly illustrate a two-pronged system of storage of gear.Oft-used tools, commonly referred to in the context of "seat tools" to ensure they are always in the seating area, can be in open shelves or hang from hooks on the walls. Tool chests, which are usually painted the colour green or blue (possibly because copper-based pigment was cheap) and are shown in numerous images of preindustrial stores. For a while, I believed they were an easy way to carry the applications of a journeyman because the man "journeyed" from shop to shop. I was wrong. The chests are huge and quite heavy.Along with the term "journeyman" can be described as the English version of the French phrase meaning "work "(Journee) that refers not about the traveling persona of this employee, however how he is paid for his work (to earn a day's wage).

These are an extremely effective method of storing hand tools. Tools are easy to find and secured from the hazards that are present in this workshop, and movable (with some effort) and the body is discreet.Made in a way that is safe The torso's lids that are tight are designed to shield the contents from corrosion. Popular Woodworking has provided several options for chests of instruments as well as walk-in closets. A benefit of having a conventional tool chest is that it could be emptying on a regular basis in the event that it is needed.If we define"seat" tools "seat tools" appropriately and with these tools are frequently used will not rust, this is not a problem. However, dramatic variations in humidity or temperature require us to reconsider the entire concept of the chair's gear. A good tool chest can create a stunning window chair or table.Tool chests of the 18th century were typically identical to blanket chests. So why not place one in your bedroom? Tools needed for the day's tasks could be removed from the chest and displayed on walls or on shelves to be returned following an evening's work, without an enormous decrease in efficiency and with a significant increase in security.

Lumber Storage Space

Hand-sawing and planing requires you to explore the grain, as well as be aware of its movements, changes in its density etc...I do not belong to the people who are enthralled by wood and its grains. But, having a thorough understanding of the material is inevitable.Before too long, every hand-tool user develops a preference for particular species of wood and inventory that is air dried instead of kiln-cooked or dried, and specific cuts of wood like plainsawn, quarter sawn heart wood, twists and so on. So, without doubt some hand-tool users that I have met purchase wood that suits their preferences, regardless of whether they will ever use it for it or not. I think it's wise if at all possible, to get ready for the long term storage of a fantastic amount of timber for future endeavors. Nonetheless, your timber rack should not automatically share your workspace. You could find your woodshed, garage or perhaps a shaded area of your backyard or garden the ideal location to put your wood rack. When you design your wood rack, consider issues as the ability to allow airflow to the stands, accessibility and protecting the timber from sun. If you have children who are part of your life routine, ensure that you have taken every precaution to keep your stand safe for children who might mistake it for a gym.

Sharpening Space

It's been suggested that the most important thing to working with hand tools is to learn how to reassemble them. The best hand tool shop has a complete inventory without features for sharpening. Although Jacques-Andre's 18th century text is filled with active sharpening area, this is not a definite requirement. The work bench could be a great place to sharpen as it's solid and is the perfect size for this type of action.However there are numerous reasons to choose having a designated area, as Robot illustrated.Most sharpening tools require some kind of lubrication that could result in a complete destruction of your seating and other jobs in the future. The grinders used by some woodworkers emit a toxic abrasive dust. Let's admit it. Sharpening is an unclean business.If you are only able to go a short distance think about a mat to safeguard your chair from water or oil that may fall off the top on your rock. The mat is dual duty.It protects your seat as well as preventing the stone from slipping around. In the case of mild emission seats, the seat could get worse but when more extensive work is needed, it's nice to have a dedicated area for sharpening. A grinder and a small table that is built in a shop and has the right size will do the trick.

The sharpening station shouldn't always be in the same place as the workshop. It may be in an unheated, unattractive location. A stifling place can discourage you from using wax. It is impossible to dissuade a woodworker quicker or more efficiently than using boring tools. When you go to the "supreme" race there may be some equipped waxing areas. The others must find a space from where we might cause a mess within.

Lighting Your Workspace

In an article written about Anthony Hay cabinet shop at Colonial Williamsburg, master cabinetmaker Mack Headley clarified a number advantages of operating under "raking" mild. The natural light from windows in the vicinity cast shadows, which allows him to be able to see the surface when planning or dividing. I've observed knife lines to disappear under the shadow-free lighting of four-foot fluorescent store lights. Shortly after my visit, Colonial Williamsburg eliminated the 4 light fixtures in my chair and began to experiment with various lighting options.

Here's what I came with. The lighting at the end of the seats is essential. While it might seem counter-intuitive the ability to turn off light off on your own can allow users to focus on what they need to see. In my chair, I'm employing a range of compact fluorescent 13-watt bulbs that are installed in clamp fittings for work lighting (they have a color temperatures of 3500K). These bulbs eliminate stunning white light, are inexpensive and, more importantly they can be switched off on their own or quickly moved to provide me with slopes at the time and place I require they. I was sure to put the lighting near the edges of the seats which is where the work is completed. It is possible to substitute traditional incandescent bulbs in fixtures that are similar or opt for the warmer and more bright halogens, however they could require unique fixtures. I found that higher-color temperatures Compact fluorescent (CF) bulbs provided superior lighting when compared to bulbs with lower colors, and they have double the power. With the lights that rake and the over-bench lights switched off, I could swiftly check if I needed to improve my writing skills.

A Stylish Shop

One of the most exciting aspects of the most trusted hand tool shop is that with some precautions, it can be secured enough to allow a baby. Woodworking is a private activity, but it ought not be. Without the sound of machines and dust of machinery, the shop might be a great location to spend time in. My store offers toys for kids (though they are a fan of cheeks made of tenon as well as plane shavings) as well as a comfy area to relax. The wood paneling didn't take much time to install however it did take away the brutality of the brick walls. The most beautiful retail store is one you're interested in. The most magnificent shop is one where your grandchild or child and their spouse or partner feel at home. The most beautiful store is one where woodworking can be shared.

Chapter 18: Easy Woodworks

While you may be able to use tools quite well but you may not have the right knowledge about how to make woodwork. As a novice it is crucial to understand how to layout or compose and complete different types of work.

These are the basic things you can begin to tackle when you are a novice in the art of woodwork and are included as enough options that will give you a base of experience and experience.You shouldn't be fooled by all the complicated variations of things that you can accomplish when you are a novice in woodworking. Try to keep it as simple as you could. There are a lot of things that you can create in the woodworking arts. You must take things one step at a time, and gain greater knowledge and experience during the process.

Make: wooden knives, swords and daggers

First, you should cut out the shape of the object you wish to create. Then, you can either round or peel it or shave it according to the thickness you require (having an axe-saw or scroll-saw can make it easier for you to spend less time creating the outline) Then, you add the final elements (sandpaper. It is suggested to create these using straight-grained wood that is easily whittled such as white pine.

How to build an animal-friendly cage (for animals)

A compact box in which you can transport a kitten, squirrel, bird, or any other small animal traveling is much more convenient than using baskets or bags. All you need to do is create a small container of 1/4 " stock. The one side should be opened (to be sealed by wire and netting later) The second side should be divided into two parts and the upper one hinged for use as a door or lid. It is possible to attach moulding strips to brads on the ends, which are where the wire will be fastened. Doorways can be hung by screw-eye and hook or catch, and an handle that is fixed to the top. If the box is going to be moved around frequently it is advised to smooth out its edges. Finally, it should be smoothed and polished.

Conclusion

I hope that this book was helpful to master the fundamentals of woodworking for beginners.

After you've read the book fully, The next thing to do is put into practice the lessons you've learned by doing a real woodworking project. This would put into the test or ultimately apply the information you've learned from the book. This guide will serve as your best friend so that you can tackle any task like a professional.

We wish you a happy and successful journey on your way!

www.ingramcontent.com/pod-product-compliance
Lightning Source LLC
Chambersburg PA
CBHW071839080526
44589CB00012B/1059